VOCABULARY BUILDER FOR ADULTS: BUSINESS VOCABULARY WORKBOOK

+ FREE DIGITAL COMPANION BOOK

+ FREE BUSINESS PLAN TEMPLATE

STUDY BUSINESS TERMINOLOGY IN USE, BUILDING COLLEGE-LEVEL VOCABULARY.

ENGLISH VOCABULARY BOOKS FOR ADULTS.

BUSINESS ENGLISH ORIGINALS SERIES

BUSINESS VOCABULARY WORKBOOK

VOCABULARY BUILDER FOR ADULTS

+ DIGITAL COMPANION BOOK

+ FREE BUSINESS PLAN TEMPLATE

Study Business Terminology in Use, Building College-Level Vocabulary

Marc Roche & IDM Business & Law

Copyright © 2020 by Marc Roche. All Right Reserved.

An earlier, more basic version of this book was originally published as *Business English Vocabulary: Advanced Masterclass* in 2018. No part of this business vocabulary book may be reproduced, distributed, or transmitted in any form or by any means, including photocopying, recording, or other electronic or mechanical methods, or by any information storage and retrieval system without the prior written permission of the publisher, except in the case of very brief quotations embodied in critical reviews and certain other noncommercial uses permitted by copyright law.

Topics covered in this book-

Business vocabulary, business English, business vocabulary builder, business English vocabulary, business vocabulary, business English writing, business English vocabulary builder, ESL advanced, ESL business English

Contents

About The Author 14

Other Business English Books by Marc Roche 15

FREE COMPANION eBOOK: "Common Investment Terms Explained" 17

FREE BUSINESS PLAN TEMPLATE 19

How to Use *Vocabulary Builder for Adults: Business Vocabulary Workbook* 21

    As a Business English Vocabulary Builder 21

    As a Business Terminology Book for Building College Level Business Vocabulary 22

    As a Vocabulary Builder for Adults (Adult Vocabulary Book, or Adult Vocabulary Workbook) 22

CHAPTER 1. CORE BUSINESS CONCEPTS 25

    'Value' in Business 26

    'Testing' a Product or Service 28

    A Niche 29

    Demographics & Customer Data 30

    Target Customers 30

    Competition 31

    Competitor Analysis 32

    Revenue 32

    Asset 33

    Net Profit 33

    Gross Profit 34

Break-Even Point 34
Cash flow 35
Fixed Costs 35
Profit Margin 36
Overheads 36
Stakeholders 37

CHAPTER 2. BUSINESS PLANNING CONCEPTS & TERMINOLOGY + FREE BUSINESS PLAN TEMPLATE 38

Mission Statement 39
    Exercise 40
The Research Phase 40
Feasibility Study 41
The Executive Summary 42
    Exercise 50
Company Description 51
    Exercise 54
Market Analysis 55
    What Goes into the Market Analysis Section of a Business Plan? 55
    Exercise 57
    NETFLIX CASE 59
    NETFLIX CASE RESOURCES 60
Marketing Strategy 63
    Product 64

Promotion	65
Price	65
Place	66
Pro Tips	67
The Customer Journey & The AIDA Principles in Marketing	**70**
Attention	71
Interest	72
Desire	73
Action	74
Buyer Persona	**76**
Needs VS Wants	77
Pro Tips	78
Exercise	79
Market Penetration: Blue Oceans & Red Oceans	**81**
Value Innovation	84
Pro Tips:	89
Exercise	90
Management Summary	**91**
Business Structure	92
Management	92
Other Individuals	93
Growth Plan	93
Pro Tips	94

- **Financial Analysis** ... 96
  - *What is in the Financial Analysis Section?* ... 97
  - *Pro Tips* ... 99
- **KEY Financial Projections** ... 102
- **Balance Sheet** ... 103
  - *How to Do the Balance Sheet* ... 103
  - *Assets* ... 105
  - *Liabilities* ... 106
  - *Equity* ... 108
- **Income statement** ... 110
- **Cash-flow statement** ... 115
- **Accounting & Finance Vocabulary Explained** ... 121
  - *Accounting Period* ... 122
  - *Annual Report* ... 123
  - *Fiscal Year* ... 124
  - *Accounts Payable* ... 124
  - *Accounts Receivable (AR)* ... 124
  - *Administration* ... 125
  - *Acquisition* ... 125
  - *Asset* ... 126
  - *Audit* ... 126
  - *Balance Sheet (BS)* ... 127
  - *Break-Even Point* ... 127
  - *Cash flow* ... 127

Creditor 128

Debtor 128

Depreciation (Dep) 128

Income Statement 129

Interim Profit Statement 129

Invoice Factoring 130

Negative Equity 130

Operating Expenditure (Operating Costs) (Opex) .131

Operating Profit/Loss 131

Present Value 131

Return on Investment 132

Rate of Return 132

FREE BUSINESS PLAN TEMPLATE 134

INVESTMENT TERMS EXPLAINED (DIGITAL COMPANION BOOK) 135

CHAPTER 4. GRAPH VOCABULARY 137

Exercise 138

Answers 144

CHAPTER 5. BAR CHART VOCABULARY 145

CHAPTER 6. PIE CHART VOCABULARY 150

Exercise One 153

Answers 154

Exercise Two 155

Answers 157

CHAPTER 7. BUSINESS DATA PRESENTED IN TABLES ..158

    Exercise One 159

    Suggested Answers: 162

CHAPTER 8. PRODUCTION PROCESSES 164

    Exercise One 166

    Exercise Two 167

    Answers 169

    Exercise Three 170

    Answers 172

CHAPTER 9. MAPS, TERRAINS & LAND DEMOGRAPHICS
....174

    Exercise One 175

    Exercise Two 178

    Exercise Three 182

    Answers 185

CHAPTER 10. MEETINGS & PUBLIC SPEAKING 188

    Exercise One 192

    Answers 195

    Referring to previous information 197

CHAPTER 11. WRITTEN BUSINESS COMMUNICATIONS 200

    LETTER OF REFERENCE 201

    Exercise One 202

    Sample Answer (Letter of Reference): 205

    Reference pronouns...207

Relative clauses 207
Substitution 207
LETTER OF COMPLAINT: 209
Paraphrasing Exercise 210
Answers 213
Topic-specific phrases 214
Ending the letter 215
Sample Answer 218
Formal Business Communication: Structure Rules ... 221
Formal Business Communication General Checklist
.... 223
Formal Business Communication: Language
Exercises 224
Exercise One 225
Answers 227
Exercise Two 229
Answers 231
Use the Passive (Sometimes) 233
6 Quick Rules of Formal VS Informal: 234
Exercise 236
Answers 238
Linking Words 239
Exercise 240
Answers 242

Informal Business Emails & Letters 243
CHAPTER 12. ESL BUSINESS ENGLISH 249
Important Phrasal Verbs for Business Communication in All Settings 251
Exercise One 259
Exercise Two 261
Answers 264
Commonly Confused Words in Business Writing 266
Business English ESL Vocabulary: Conversations (Speaking Phrases) 273
CHAPTER 13. LEARN 2,500 NEW BUSINESS WORDS IN 6 MONTHS. 277
Method 1: Mnemonic Devices 278
Method 2: FANBOYS 278
Method 3: The Tongue Twister Method 279
Method 3: Teach The Mirror Method 280
Method 4: Hack Your Routine 281
Method 5: Notecards or post-it notes 281
Method 6: Use Suffixes 282
Method 7: Read, Read, and Read! 283
Method 8: The 30-Minute Rule 284
Method 9: The Newspaper Method 285
Method 10: The Interaction Method 285
Method 11: The Chunking Method 286

FREE EBOOK: "Common Investment Terms Explained"
....288
FREE BUSINESS PLAN TEMPLATE 290
The End & Special Thank You..292

About The Author

Marc has been a business writing coach and an academic English exam prep specialist for over ten years. He has collaborated with organizations such as the British Council, the Royal Melbourne Institute of Technology (RMIT), University of Technology Sydney, and multinationals such as Nike, GlaxoSmithKline, and Bolsas y Mercados, among others.

OTHER BUSINESS ENGLISH BOOKS BY MARC ROCHE

Business English Writing: Advanced Masterclass- How to Communicate Effectively & Communicate with Confidence: How to Write Emails, Business Letters & Business Reports. Includes 100+ Business Letters

Business Email: Write to Win!

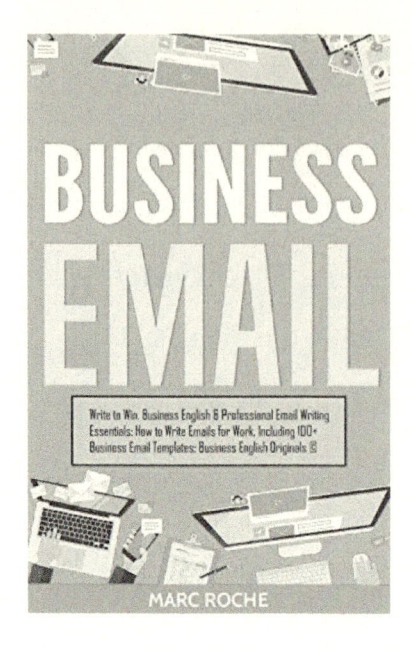

FREE COMPANION eBOOK:

"COMMON INVESTMENT TERMS EXPLAINED"

Sign up to the FREE VIP List today to grab your FREE downloadable eBook ☺

Details can be found at the end of the book.

FREE BUSINESS PLAN TEMPLATE

Access your **FULL FREE Business Plan Template** in the Business Plan Template section and at the back of the book!

This book can be used in several ways, depending on your specific objectives.

How to Use *Vocabulary Builder for Adults: Business Vocabulary Workbook*

As a Business English Vocabulary Builder

Business English vocabulary is essential to speak about, write about, and understand business concepts. However, it is also the key that will allow you to research business-related topics and gain more specific knowledge of finance, strategy, economics, and many other areas. Gaining an understanding of key business vocabulary with this adult vocabulary builder will also vastly improve your written English and speaking skills, as well as your listening comprehension.

AS A BUSINESS TERMINOLOGY BOOK FOR BUILDING COLLEGE LEVEL BUSINESS VOCABULARY

"Vocabulary Builder for Adults: Business Vocabulary Workbook. Study Business Terminology in Use" is a business terminology book for building college-level business vocabulary. Learn the vocabulary needed to describe data, lead meetings, and ace presentations.

AS A VOCABULARY BUILDER FOR ADULTS (ADULT VOCABULARY BOOK, OR ADULT VOCABULARY WORKBOOK)

This vocabulary builder for adults is packed with business vocabulary, including specialized exercises and explanations. *"Vocabulary Builder for Adults: Business Vocabulary Workbook. Study Business Terminology in Use. Building College Level Vocabulary"* contains essential business language, with exercises for professional settings and business English conversation vocabulary for meetings and presentations.

"Vocabulary Builder for Adults: Business Vocabulary Workbook.." is an ideal adult vocabulary book for anyone who has problems understanding, remembering, and using business English vocabulary and for anyone who wants to communicate more confidently in the business world. Don't waste hours researching words and trying to understand their meanings. This book will make your learning more efficient with less of your own effort, which means more spare time to review other concepts.

The review and consolidation exercises also make it the perfect adult vocabulary workbook. It will give you the skills, tools, knowledge, and practice needed to feel confident when presenting and writing business-related information. This business vocabulary book is a step-by-step self-study manual on how to use and understand business terminology. Knowing this vocabulary will help prepare you for all the situations in your professional life.

The vocabulary included is essential for:

- ✓ Adult vocabulary building
- ✓ Business Plans
- ✓ Understanding business concepts and core principles
- ✓ Business terminology for university and college
- ✓ Building college-level vocabulary
- ✓ Describing data
- ✓ Leading meetings
- ✓ Acing Presentations
- ✓ Business English vocabulary building
- ✓ Learning business terminology

CHAPTER 1. CORE BUSINESS CONCEPTS

'Value' in Business

Ask yourself about your company's core values and what purpose the company serves. How does it 'bring value' to people? Providing value should arguably be at the core of any business objectives or business plan.

Will you be aiming to reduce the wait times for daycares in your community? Will you provide a place for customers to enjoy locally-made pasta dishes? Is it an Internet café in a community where there are no options for those without computers?

Knowing the purpose of your business will ensure that you have a compass for the decisions you will make in the future. It also provides you with an excellent starting point for meetings, negotiations, business plans, and emails.

Within this question of your business's purpose are two other very important questions.

- WHY:

Why does your company exist?

Why will people buy your product or service?

Why will you and/or your employees get out of bed in the morning to work and make your company successful?

- HOW:

How will you and your employees or colleagues, if you have any, represent your company to its customers?

How will the values of the company translate to success in the community?

How will your customers or clients know what you stand for?

'Testing' a Product or Service

Whether it is a service or product, you need to at least test out your idea before launching. This is like creating a prototype before you start selling anything.

Maybe you want to open a coffee shop, but you test out the response to your coffee by providing it to friends and family and seeing what they think. You should talk to potential customers in your market and other entrepreneurs to see how viable the idea is. You should speak to industry experts and other experts to get their honest feedback.

This is about constructive criticism. You may want to open a coffee shop, but after talking to an expert or potential customer, your idea may evolve, and you may come up with a better concept, which serves a particular niche.

A Niche

A niche is a specific group of people who like a certain thing, or in other words, a specific part of the market.

Talking with others and putting the idea out there will help you know the market, who will buy, and who competes in that market.

You can even test your product or service and find your niche by creating social media and website profiles, combining them with social media ads, and testing and measuring the response against your target market. [Gary Vaynerchuk](#) advocates this technique, as it saves you a lot of time and money, and it stops you from wasting your precious time creating products that no one will buy. If, for some reason, you haven't heard of Gary Vaynerchuk, I'd wholeheartedly recommend that you watch a few of his videos and consume some of his content.

Demographics & Customer Data

Any relevant information relating to your customers and their region is classed as demographics. Age, gender, level of education, income, interests, race, ethnicity/ cultural background, religion, marital status, region of the country, etc.

Target Customers

Your target customer is the specific section of the market (or niche) who would be interested in your product or service. The general recommendation here is to try to be as specific as possible when deciding who they are.

What are the demographics of your customers or clients? You should ensure that you know the area your business serves, who lives there, and what their habits are.

COMPETITION

The competition you will face is very important unless you offer something truly unique. You have to be honest with yourself here. Unique isn't just unique because you say so. It has to be a truly different and memorable product or experience.

Going back to the coffee shop scenario, if there are ten coffee shops in a 20-block radius, then a coffee shop might not be your best option for a business unless you can offer an experience that customers want and can't get in the other coffee shops. This is where you can carry out a Competitor Analysis!

Competitor Analysis

It isn't just about how many businesses like yours are in your area. It is also about researching their products and services. Maybe there are a bunch of coffee shops, but none offer free-trade coffee. If that is the case, you have a niche you can fill, especially in a neighborhood where something like that is important to the consumer. This is where research comes in and why it is so important.

Revenue

Revenues come from the sale of products, merchandise, and services. Revenues also include earnings from interest and dividend payments made to shareholders or rent received for property ownership.

Asset

Assets are a company's most valuable resource. They represent the fruits of past transactions and events and anything legally claimed by the business, such as money or property rights in another person's name (like intellectual properties). An asset is something with economic value to its owner; it has future benefits too!

Net Profit

Net Profit is the revenue generated after taking off all costs. Net Income or Net Profit helps determine overall profitability, reflecting how effectively the business has managed its assets to generate profit.

Gross Profit

Gross Profit is the measure of a company's profitability without accounting for overhead expenses. It can be calculated by subtracting the Cost of Goods Sold from Revenue for that same period, making it a critical indicator of future success!

Break-Even Point

The break-even point is where total revenues are equal to total costs. It's an essential concept because it can help you figure out whether or not your business will be profitable, at least in the short term.

Cash flow

Cash flow is the money that enters and leaves a business. The Net Cash Flow for a period can be found by taking the Initial Cash Balance and subtracting the Closing Balance.

Fixed Costs

Fixed costs, like rent and salaries, won't change if the company sells more. The opposite of Fixed Costs is Variable Costs. Variable Costs can vary according to how many times they're used or produced per unit period; for example, wages may increase with increased production rates due to the payment of overtime or due to the employment of extra temporary staff to meet the increase in demand. This variable cost would decrease when there was less work needed.

Profit Margin

A company's profit margin is the percentage of each sale that results in net income. A high number means the business is having an easier time making money. In contrast, a low number suggests it might be difficult for them to turn enough revenue into profits, perhaps due to competition from other companies offering similar products or services with lower prices overall.

Overheads

Overheads are business costs that we cannot trace to a specific cost unit or activity, but instead, we must pay on an ongoing basis regardless of whether we are selling products or not. Examples of this are insurance, rent, and utility bills.

STAKEHOLDERS

Anyone with a vested interest in a business. For instance, this can be shareholders, managers, directors, staff, or suppliers.

CHAPTER 2. BUSINESS PLANNING CONCEPTS & TERMINOLOGY + FREE BUSINESS PLAN TEMPLATE

Mission Statement

When you need to write a business plan, you need to know what your mission statement will be. Your mission statement is essential, and it comes down to summarizing in one sentence why your company is in business and why customers will buy from you. The mission statement is a concise way to translate your entire business plan into one or two sentences! Your mission statement is your vision for the company and what you want to accomplish.

Note: Before you start, outline five different strategies that will help you accomplish what you plan to achieve.

EXERCISE

Step 1. Choose any company and write a short mission statement for it, based on the information you've read so far.

Step 2. Check the examples as a loose guideline: https://www.idmbusinessenglish.com/business-plan-answers

THE RESEARCH PHASE

When you want to create a company that sells a product or a service, you always need to conduct research. This applies directly to the Product Testing section in the Core Business Concepts Chapter.

Always ask yourself, "have we tested it?" You need to research everything about your business idea because that's the only way you will ever know if it is going to be successful or not.

Feasibility Study

The feasibility study analyses the main elements of a business plan: your idea, the advantage you have over your competition, an avatar of your ideal customer, and your daily activities. You should also have realistic numbers to predict your cash flows. We will look at all of these concepts later in the book, so don't worry.

By writing up and then reading through your feasibility plan, you'll quickly see if your initial idea is sound enough to go forward with or not.

THE EXECUTIVE SUMMARY

The opening section of a business plan is one of the most important parts because it can win or lose your reader.

When you look at the back of a book, you get a brief idea of what the book is about. The executive summary functions similarly by giving an overview of your business.

People are busy, and their time is precious, so you need to respect that. Your reader will get an impression of you and your business from the opening section, and if the first impression is negative, it's tough to reverse.

The Executive Summary is a snapshot of your whole business, and it needs to fit perfectly with the rest of the plan.

Paragraph 1 should say the problem you will solve for your customers or clients and why you're different from your competitors.

Paragraph 2 should say who your target customers are, who your competitors are and how much money you expect to make.

Then you need to write a short part about your staff or team. Who will you need to work with? Give some details about skills and experience.

The final paragraph needs to focus on finances, with:

- ✓ Projected income (the money you predict will come into the business) for at least the first year, preferably the first 2-3 years.
- ✓ You should also detail how much money you need to start the business or venture.
- ✓ How much will you (or your company) contribute?
- ✓ How much will lenders or investors contribute?

The maximum length for the executive summary

The maximum length for the executive summary should typically be two pages (at the very most), so remember to keep it concise and clear. It's also probably best to write this section last, as you'll have a better idea of what to say and how to say it once you've written the other sections.

The Executive Summary should summarize the business plan so that someone looking at it will get a quick idea of what you are selling, what you need from them, and how you will succeed.

The executive summary must be very clear and concise. Don't get bogged down in information that will bore the reader. Get to the point and impress the reader from the start.

Therefore, you should think of the executive summary as one of the most critical parts of the entire business plan. It is the cover of the book; it is the trailer to the film; it is what sells the business plan before you sell the idea to the reader!

What Goes in an Executive Summary?

The executive summary isn't a one-paragraph analysis of your company. It is a detailed look at your entire business plan in a summarized form. The following are some headings you could use to help the reader understand your business from the start.

- The Opportunity: What is the need for your product or service in the community or area? What opportunity does this present?

- Advantage: How will your business take advantage of the existing opportunity?

- The Market: Who is the market that will buy the product or service? Will you create a new market?

- Business Model: What is your product or service, and what will make it something the target market will go after?

- Marketing Strategy: How will you market your product or service? Describe briefly.

- Competition: Who else is in the market, and how will you get a market share or create a new market? Do you have a competitive advantage over other businesses? Can you offer customers something that they cannot get from your competitors?

- Financial Analysis: This is just a quick summary of the financial plan. You should have brief projections for income and expenses for the next two to three years.

- Owners: Who owns the company, how are they qualified, and why will they make the business successful? You can also outline your staff in this area and how they will help the company.

- Plan Implementation: How will you take your company from this moment to opening its doors and beyond.

Other things that you can include, depending on where your business is in its planning stages, are:

- Mission Statement: What is the purpose of your business, and what is its philosophy.

- Company Info: Give a brief history of the company here. This applies more to an established business looking to expand.

- Business Highlights: Like Company Info, this is for a business that has begun to establish itself. If you have had success in the market and are now going into business for yourself, you can include your highlights here.

- Future Goals: Where do you see the company going? What goals do you have for the company?

Tips for Writing the Executive Summary

You should focus on just giving a summary since that is literally what this section is called. Don't go into super detail with everything. Don't waste the time of the reader. Keep it a summary because you go into greater detail later.

You need to make sure you keep positive language in your summary. That may seem self-explanatory, but it is a common pitfall. Instead of saying, "With funding, the company should be able to find success." Seems okay, right? It's not. It is not favorable, and it tells the reader the company and its staff are not sure of themselves. Instead, you should say, "The company will be in an excellent position to dominate the market share and will find even more success with the proper funding."

Remember that the Executive Summary should ideally be around two pages at most. It is a summary, so don't forget, so don't pad things out. Get to the point and move on.

EXERCISE

Step 1. Download the FREE Business Plan Template from https://www.idmbusinessenglish.com/free-business-plan-template

Step 2. Choose a company you will write about, and complete the "Executive Summary" section of the template using the guidelines provided. Remember to use as much vocabulary from this section as possible.

Step 3. Check the example as a loose guideline: https://www.idmbusinessenglish.com/business-plan-answers

COMPANY DESCRIPTION

In this section of a business plan, you are describing your company, so you should include:

- ✓ **Company Name:** This must be the official name of your business as it is registered.
- ✓ **Type of Business**: Is your business an LLC or a corporation? Is it a partnership or a sole proprietorship/sole trader or equivalent? This is essential information for the reader if you seek investment or joint ventures.
- ✓ **Owners**: Who are the people behind the company, and what is their experience? How will they bring success to the company?
- ✓ **Location**: Where is your company located? Does it have multiple locations? Do you have a headquarters for the company?

- ✓ **History**: This may not be very long if you are a new small business, but you can still go into detail about the company and how the idea for it came about. What inspired you to create the business? Let your passion tell the history.
- ✓ **Product/Service**: So, what are you selling? Why are you selling it? Give a brief overview of the product or service and who you want to sell it to.
- ✓ **Objectives**: This just details your immediate future goals for the company and how you will achieve them.

Tips for Writing the Company Description

The first paragraph in your company description part should capture all the information about the company. You are essentially pitching your company here, so keep it quick and concise, but show your passion for the business and why you believe in it so much.

You will have a lot of information about your company, the staff, and the product later in the business plan, so you should keep only the most critical information in this section. Give a general overview of the information without going into too much detail.

Show your passion for your company and let it transfer to the business plan and this section. You don't want to produce another boring business plan that investors, lenders, and potential partners will have to wade through or even throw in the trash. Be yourself, be authentic, be original and be professional at the same time.

This section shouldn't be too long, maybe one to two pages. You should read through everything and cut out any information that doesn't need to be there.

EXERCISE

Step 1. If you haven't already, download the FREE Business Plan Template from https://www.idmbusinessenglish.com/free-business-plan-template

Step 2. Write about the same company you chose for your Executive Summary in the previous section. Complete the "Company Description" section using the guidelines provided.

Remember to use as much vocabulary from this book as possible!

Step 3. There are no suggested answers for this, as every description will differ. The purpose of this activity is for you to practice describing your business using the language and concepts you've learned so far!

Market Analysis

Understanding the industry you are getting into is vitally important if you want your company to succeed.

What Goes into the Market Analysis Section of a Business Plan?

In this section, you can divide the information into the following parts.

- **Industry Description/Outlook**: This section will look at the industry you are starting your business in. It is where you will address the sector's size, its growth, where the trends are, and what the outlook of the industry happens to be.

- **Target Customer** (Ideal Customer): Who will you target with your product or service? Who is the customer that you want to reach? The information in this section must dive deep into the demographics of the customer group you are trying to reach. This must include the age range of your ideal customer, their income level, and what type of lifestyle they lead. In addition to this information, you should also look at the purchase potential of the individual customer, what their motivations are for buying your product and how you are going to reach that customer. It helps to give them a name so that you can 'humanize' them as much as possible.

- **Market Test**: If you are going to release your product or service, you need to carry out some initial hard evidence about the market you're targeting. This is where you put the investigation results, including how you tested out the market and all the supporting statistics. Be honest and impartial, don't lie to yourself here.

- Lead Time: This is a vital section because it will detail the time it will take for any order to be completed. When your customer makes a purchase, how long will it take them to receive the finished product or service? How will you handle individual orders? How will you handle large volume purchases?

- Analysis of Competition: Who will be competing with you in the market? What are the strengths of the competition? What are their weaknesses? How will you outperform them? What are the problems standing in your way to keep you from competing against that competition?

EXERCISE

Step 1. If you haven't already, download the FREE Business Plan Template from https://www.idmbusinessenglish.com/free-business-plan-template

Step 2. Write about the same company you chose for the previous sections. Complete the "Market Analysis" section of the template using the guidelines provided.

Remember to use as much vocabulary from this book as possible!

Step 3. There are no suggested answers for this, as the purpose of this activity is for you to practice describing your market using the vocabulary and concepts you've learned so far!

NETFLIX CASE

Analyzing the market will keep you on the cutting edge. The market analysis section looks at these types of trends and explains to those reading the business plan where you see the market going and how your product or service will succeed. It provides a detailed overview of the industry, and you will have to have statistics within the section to back up everything you say.

The market analysis section will look at the industry, the market you are going to target, the competition in that market, and where your product or service will be situated in the market. If you have a lot of data to back up your claims in this section, that should be provided in the appendices at the end of the business plan.

When Netflix started, there was no real media streaming. High-speed internet was very new, and people still rented their content, bought it in physical form, or downloaded it illegally. Netflix latched onto this idea, and while they provided physical copies at first, they looked at the market and saw that it was moving in the direction of streaming. When the time came, Netflix shifted quickly, and now the company is worth billions. On the other hand, Blockbuster was an iconic household brand loved by millions of people worldwide. Still, they did not see the shift coming, or did not react in time, arguably due to poor leadership, and now sadly, they're gone forever.

NETFLIX CASE RESOURCES

The following NY Times article from 2007 announcing Netflix's plan to offer online movies and series gives you a good feel for what the video rental market looked like back then:

Netflix to Deliver Movies to the PC

By Miguel Helft (January 16, 2007)

https://www.nytimes.com/2007/01/16/technology/16netflix.html

In the following 2018 article, Ted Sarandos details how Netflix predicted the market and went with it rather than resisting the changes.

Ted Sarandos on How Netflix Predicted the Future of TV

By Cynthia Littleton, Janko Roettgers (Aug 21, 2018)

https://variety.com/2018/digital/news/netflix-streaming-dvds-original-programming-1202910483/

If you are interested in reading about this topic in more detail, you can access the following Case Study by the U.S. think tank New America.

Case Study: Netflix

New America

https://www.newamerica.org/oti/reports/why-am-i-seeing-this/case-study-netflix/

MARKETING STRATEGY

You've shown what the market is like. You've analyzed it and presented your findings clearly and concisely. Now it's time to show how you're going to get into that market, or in business-speak 'penetrate the market,' and make a profit.

The marketing strategy part of a business plan builds on what the market analysis section already delved into. In this part of the business plan, you outline where your business will sit in the market, how you will price your product or service, and how you will sell and promote it.

Your marketing strategy shows you, vendors, investors, and employees how you plan to sell your product or service. It will also show future marketing ideas you have. There are several essential parts to the market strategy section.

Product

In this part of the market strategy section, you need to explain your product and why it will sell in the market. This includes explaining the brand name, any products or services related to it, and its functionality. In the product area, you need to explain the quality of the finished product, what the warranty will be for it, and even the packaging it will be sold in. This should be a more scientific description of the product or service than what we looked at in previous sections.

PROMOTION

This part covers the various aspects of how you will market your product or service. In this section, you will address what your marketing budget will be, the promotional strategy, and any publicity you plan for it. This also includes the advertising, who your sales force is and why they are qualified, and how you will handle sales promotions.

PRICE

The price you charge for your product or service is incredibly important. Charge too much, and you won't sell anything. Charge too little, and you won't bring enough money in to be sustainable. Some things to address in the price section are how you will bundle the product or service with other products and services your company sells. You also need to explain how flexible you are on the price and what your pricing strategy is going to be. The retail price should be addressed and how you came to that number. In addition to the retail price, you need to address the seasonal price of your product if it is applicable and any wholesale prices you may offer for larger volume orders.

PLACE

- How are you going to deliver your product or service to the customer?
- Will you have distribution centers or distribution channels?
- How will you handle inventory management and the logistics of the orders if you're selling physical products?
- How will you process the orders?
- Do you need a transportation network?
- Will you be keeping the product in a warehouse?
- Will you distribute your product or service through the Internet, by truck, or another distribution method?

PRO TIPS

If you are more about ideas and managing, determining a marketing strategy may seem like a daunting task. To make it easier, I've compiled some tips to help get your marketing strategy off the ground and ready to roll.

The first thing you need to do is ensure that your marketing strategy is unique in some way.

Let's look at PayPal. When they first started, they literally paid customers if they referred someone. After a few months, they paid less for referrals until they had finally ended the program after a few years, spending tens of millions of dollars. That allowed the company to expand its customer base heavily, and it's now a company worth billions. To make your strategy unique, you should have a unique selling proposition. This is how you will explain how your marketing differs from other companies in your industry.

Be flexible with your marketing strategy.

Try different things, let some things stick and others not. Don't be afraid to try out some promotional ideas in your business plan that are way out of the box and some that are standard. Do your research and don't expect any one method to make you millions overnight; it's all a learning curve.

When you determine your pricing, you should have the data to back up why you are pricing the product for that specific amount.

Include ads from your competition, reports from the industry, and any research you have conducted yourself.

The marketing strategy should use visuals if possible.

Include charts, graphs, and anything that gets the information and facts out in a way that will be easier for your reader to understand.

Do not forget about your budget when doing your marketing strategy section.

Keep in mind the numbers from your financial analysis and translate that into how you will budget the promotion of your company and make a profit based on the price. You need to tie it into your financial status.

The Customer Journey & The AIDA Principles in Marketing

The buyer journey is the process that someone goes through before buying from you. If you have enough social proof through reviews etc.. and you look legitimate, people might purchase from you without you necessarily seeing the journey they've gone through before making that purchase.

In other words, you might not have directly interacted with them as much, but they'll still have done some research on you after noticing you, and they will have had contact with your brand several times.

When you understand this buyer journey, you can plan your marketing around it.

ATTENTION

The first part of the buyer journey is *attention*. This is the first time you notice something.

Physical Example

Imagine you need a pair of trainers (sneakers), and you notice some nice ones in a shop window or on social media. This would be the 'attention' phase of your journey as a customer.

Online Example

This is the part of the buyer journey where you apply social media marketing.

Social media marketers often make their content:

Dramatic

Interesting

Sometimes controversial

Eye-catching

INTEREST

Physical Example

The trainers you've just noticed cost 200 USD, but they've been reduced to 100 USD. You have 100 USD to spend. Your mind has already started to intellectualize it and justify the purchase because, after all, you can afford these trainers.

Online Example

If you are doing business online, at this stage, you're aiming to engage the customer's mind and establish yourself as an expert in your field. Educating for free is an excellent way to gain expert status in your customers' minds. It helps them trust you because you provide quality and value for free.

A great way to create content like this is to use FAQs. FAQs can help solve common issues your clients encounter. People who approach your business will often come more informed and be easier to sell to. Since they've been in touch with your business, you've provided them with value, and they have fewer questions.

Whenever possible, try to create content that doesn't go out of date. This way, you're building long-term assets to recruit customers. This is called 'evergreen' content.

Desire

Physical Example

You try the trainers on, and you like the way they look, or you look at pictures online and like the style. You imagine yourself wearing them. Desire kicks in. You want the trainers now.

Online Example

In this stage, the customer has made a small commitment like giving you their email. This is intimate, and you can now talk to them privately. Within your newsletters, there should be an offer where they can take action. You want to create desire. They need to feel that you have a close relationship. It has to be personal.

ACTION

Physical Example

On your way out of the shop, a shop assistant asks you if you want the trainers. This is a call to action. You decide that it's something you like and can afford, so you buy.

Online Example

Here is where you ask for people to decide. Online, this could be a pop-up or an email if you have the customer's email address. It could also be done through a retargeting ad on Facebook or Google, for example. You don't need to be spammy; you're asking for a decision on a fair deal. You should offer them exclusive discounts in your newsletter and show them your entry-level products before you market more expensive items to them.

BUYER PERSONA

Creating a fictional ideal buyer persona and giving them a name may sound silly, but it's going to help when it comes to marketing. You can draw a picture of a person and write down their age and relationship status. Do they have kids? What type of lifestyle does your character have? Income? Where do they live? What are their hobbies?

Write it all down. It's essential to have a clear idea of who your perfect customer is.

What is your buyer trying to buy?

If you have a business selling bottled water, your customer isn't trying to buy water. The chances are, they have plenty of tap water at home already. If your customers are middle-class professionals living in the city, they might be interested in convenience, health, and image. Focus on the benefits that your customers are interested in buying instead of the features of the product. Nobody likes to pay for expensive water; they want to feel healthy with convenient on-the-go products that look good or avoid disease.

Another example might be if you're selling toasters. Customers might want a budget toaster, or a status toaster or an ultra-safe toaster or an eco-toaster, and so on. Once you start to look at this, you can narrow down your marketing and strategy to reach the right customers with the right type of products.

Needs VS Wants

Understanding the buyer persona will lead you to their wants. People buy what they want, not what they need. Once a customer desires your product or service, they'll then try to justify it with logic. Take, for example, a Mercedes Benz. Does anyone need one? Wouldn't a cheaper car be just as valuable for anyone needing to get around? Would you be able to find a vehicle that is as reliable and efficient as a Mercedes for less money? The answer is probably yes, but that's irrelevant when you want a Mercedes.

Pro Tips

One of the biggest problems customers have is that they can't understand businesses. When someone has specialist knowledge in an area, they often start to communicate using jargon, expecting everyone to understand. To your customers, it's like you're speaking a different language. When you're trying to communicate with your customers effectively, you have to translate your industry-speak to something they can understand. One of the most important skills a professional in any field can have is translating technical language into simple terms.

In some cases, customers might have the technical knowledge to have in-depth conversations about your product or service. Still, in most cases, even in business-to-business, you need to focus on solving problems!

For example, *X does Y*

EXERCISE

Step 1. Use the FREE template:

https://www.idmbusinessenglish.com/free-business-plan-template

Step 2. Practice the vocabulary and concepts learned so far. Complete the "Organization & Management" section of the template using the guidelines provided.

Remember to use as much vocabulary from this book as possible!

Market Penetration: Blue Oceans & Red Oceans

The idea of a "Blue Ocean Strategy" was first used by Professors Chan Kim and Renée Mauborgne. They introduced the concepts of *red* and *blue oceans* in their international best-seller <u>Blue Ocean Strategy</u>.

If you haven't read this book yet, I highly recommend that you do.

The idea is that markets with fierce competition and low-profit margins are "red oceans," where it is challenging to prosper, and strategy centers around beating your competition. Some companies break away from these markets and create their own markets where competition becomes irrelevant and strategy centers around creating value through innovation.

You can discover a blue ocean by concentrating on the factors that matter to customers/clients while ignoring factors they don't care about. This attracts a new type of customer that wouldn't have bought from you in many cases. The tricky part is identifying an effective strategy and carrying it out successfully.

A lot of mainstream business strategy in the 80s, 90s and 00s was primarily preoccupied with the competition. Michael

Porter's five forces and the SWOT analysis focus mainly on the environment of the business and its competitors. In these red oceans, market structures are well known and predetermined by the past, as companies attempt to beat their competitors to acquire customers within the existing market. After a while, these markets become saturated, and products and services become interchangeable commodities that compete on price. As a result of this ecosystem, profits drop, and companies become stagnant.

The situation is made worse by technological breakthroughs in production and delivery, allowing for more efficient supply, outstripping demand, and allowing businesses to keep competing on price.

You need a strategy that creates a new market space, a new type of demand, and profitable growth. The market structure has not been established yet in this type of environment.

VALUE INNOVATION

When Renée A. Mauborgne and W. Chan Kim analyzed strategic moves over 120 years, they found that the pursuit of value innovation was at the core of successful new market creation strategies.

They also found that creating value without innovation leads to progressive improvements without creating new market spaces or niches. A good example is a business that reduces costs and prices by 3.5%. This is a fantastic improvement for the company and its customers, and it creates a lot of value. However, this won't directly lead to a new market space being created or to the business standing out from its competitors in the long term.

Similarly, pushing innovation without adding value will often lead a business to focus too much on new technologies and pioneering at customers' expense. It's important to remember that you are here to serve customers and that being a pioneer in the sector must come with a customer focus. Webvan is arguably a good example of this type of mistake. You can find an interesting article on this at techcrunch.com https://techcrunch.com/2013/09/27/why-webvan-failed-and-how-home-delivery-2-0-is-addressing-the-problems/

The ideal balance is arguably to try to do things innovatively while still delivering a breakthrough in value to your customers or clients.

New gaps are constantly being created in different markets. The aviation industry, the film industry, and the healthcare industry didn't exist in the 1900s. In the 1970s, e-commerce, smartphones, biotechnology, and coffee shops weren't industries either.

If you focus on the existing market without any regard for innovation and value, you are not playing to the ever-changing reality of the market. New sectors will pop up in the next 10-20 years, and billions of dollars will be made. There are massive opportunities out there.

According to Renée A. Mauborgne and W. Chan Kim, in the study of 108 new business launches by existing companies, 86% were incremental extensions of existing markets. Still, they only accounted for 62% of revenues and 39% of profits. On the other hand, only 14% of launches created new market spaces, providing 38% of total revenues and 61% of profits.

While this data suggests that creating new market spaces can be extremely profitable, it is easy to forget that they may be riskier, as you are entering unchartered territory

Focusing on creating new market spaces can be very rewarding and profitable but work-intensive. With this strategy, you create an untapped marketplace beyond the pre-established market boundaries.

Instead of finding ways to squeeze in and compete with established businesses, you are trying to find customers or clients who have been ignored by the sector or are currently underserved. Think of Netflix, for example, and how it used the traditional video rental market, combined with the neglected illegal internet download market. It provided a happy medium, whereby, for a small monthly fee, people who used to rent videos and DVDs could now watch programs online. It simultaneously attracted illegal downloaders, who were happy to pay for a service in exchange for convenience and safety (fast, accessible, legal, and no viruses).

Like Netflix has done, by expanding your efforts in value and innovation, you could potentially reach more consumers or clients and eliminate a large part of the competition at the same time.

Another example of this type of strategy is Starbucks. Starbuck was by no stretch of the imagination the first coffee shop or even arguably the best.

When Starbuck arrived on the scene, dozens of coffee shops were more established. Instead of focusing on the coffee, Starbucks worked on branding itself as a different kind of experience to your run-of-the-mill coffee shop. They reached an untapped level of consumers by offering high-priced coffee, teas, smoothies, and Frappuccino. They also offered WIFI and sold CDs and newspapers, encouraging coffee lovers to stay around and chat. This allowed Starbucks to become a social venue and workplace for freelancers worldwide.

PRO TIPS:

Questions you can ask yourself to help you identify new opportunities.

- ✓ Is the market ready for my product or service?
- ✓ Is it ahead of its time, or is it the right time to launch it?
- ✓ Would it be cost-effective to produce your product or service at the moment, or would it cost too much?
- ✓ How much has it cost similar businesses to get up and running? This is vital.

EXERCISE

Step 1. Use the FREE template:

https://www.idmbusinessenglish.com/free-business-plan-template

Step 2. Write about your company to practice the vocabulary and concepts you've learned so far. Complete the "Marketing and Sales" section of the template using the guidelines provided.

Remember to use as much vocabulary from this book as possible!

Management Summary

Think of your business as a ship, and the ship has a crew. You have the map that will guide you to success, but you need someone to help steer and manage the day-to-day maintenance of that ship. This is where the management team comes in. They are the crew, and a good crew will make your business successful.

In the management summary section of a business plan, you outline the management team and how they will make your business successful. This section backs up everything you have said in the business plan by showing your team of experts and the resources you have behind you. You need to plan which jobs would be best done by other people. They could do the job in person if your business requires it, or remotely, like virtual assistants, content managers, etc.

BUSINESS STRUCTURE

What type of business do you have? Is it a partnership? Is it just you? Have you registered as a corporation? This is all outlined in this part.

MANAGEMENT

If you're a solopreneur, then this would be just you. However, if you've got other people involved, then; who is the team managing the company? If you have formed your company into a corporation, who will sit on the directors. In this part, you would probably want to include an organizational chart that outlines who manages what in the company.

OTHER INDIVIDUALS

Other than your board and your employees, what other support do you have externally in the company? This includes your accountants, professionals who handle your public relations, administrative support, and attorneys. If you're a one-man band, you need to outline who will help you with the different parts of the business. Do you have a content manager, a virtual assistant, an accountant?

GROWTH PLAN

In this section, you will look at the employees' salaries in the company over the next few years. This gives a clear indication of your current and future payroll costs.

Pro Tips

Of all the sections in the business plan, the management summary is probably the easiest to write in many cases. It's a very important section, though, since it analyzes the potential of the company and the employees in it.

- **Explain Things**: In this part, you want to describe how the employees in the company interact with each other. Go into a bit more detail beyond what your organizational chart says. How do roles cross over? Who handles multiple aspects of the company's operations?

- **Relate Experience**: How does the experience of each employee relate to the role they play in the business? Does the person handling the accounting have a strong background in accounting? Is your IT person someone with a lot of experience? These things sound obvious, but it's easy to assume things and then pay the price when you're wrong if you don't plan them.

- **Keep It Simple**: Don't go into too much detail about the biographical information of the employees. If you want to put in full biographies of everyone, you can do that in the appendix.

- **Everyone Is Involved**: If you have employees, partners, or managers, you want to make sure that everyone has a look at this section. Let them read what you have said about them. They may add extra details to what you have already said in the business plan. This also ensures what you say is accurate.

Financial Analysis

In this incredibly important section, you want to make sure that you outline all the data for the financing of your business.

Questions You Should Answer:

- ✓ What will your business need to expand and grow?
- ✓ What are the estimated operating expenses of your business?

If you don't have a background in finance, then it might be a good idea to hire a financial advisor to handle this or an accountant. **Having accurate data is incredibly important here, so you want to make sure that a qualified person handles this section if possible. Still, you also need to understand the principles yourself to handle the reality of your business.**

WHAT IS IN THE FINANCIAL ANALYSIS SECTION?

Within this section, you will delve deep into your business's finances. It could be very dry reading for some. Still, it is vitally important to ensure that your business is successful and that you are giving people an accurate representation of not only where your company is now but where it's going!

-Balance Sheet: You should have a rundown of your finances, including any equity the business has, any liabilities, and all assets.

-**Cash Flow Analysis:** This looks at the cash coming into the company based on what you forecast the sales of your product or service will be. You then subtract the expenses of running the business. This provides you with a cash flow analysis.

-**Profit-Loss Analysis**: This is an income statement, which takes the costs of the business activities minus the earnings over a specified period.

-**Break-Even Analysis:** What is the cost of doing business? This is always a vital question, and a break-even analysis looks at the point where sales cover the cost of doing business. How much does your company need to stay in business without losing money but not gaining any money?

Personnel Expenses: If it applies, what are your team's expenses? How much does it cost to get them everything that they need?

PRO TIPS

These tips can help make it easier for you to navigate the tricky financial section if you're not a numbers person.

- ✓ Keep it Realistic!

    The numbers you include in these statements must be supported by solid proof. The proof can be from historical data, market research, or any credible source as long as it's logical. Some people even draft a 'worst-case scenario' version and a conservatively optimistic version to see both ends of the spectrum. If you do this, just change your assumptions about the key numbers so that the calculations are as accurate as possible.

- ✓ Make good assumptions.

    It's all about making informed guesses. Don't be afraid to make some assumptions over where you see the company going in terms of its finances. When forecasting, the most important thing is to keep things consistent and allow yourself and other potential investors to make informed decisions based on sound data.

Again, you might need some help with this section after doing the initial statements. To lower the stress of figuring out financials, have a professional come in and help.

- ✓ Remember in this section to include where the data comes from and what the numbers mean. Don't forget about the generally accepted accounting principles, a collection of rules that define accepted accounting practice.

- ✓ Make sure your math is accurate. One small mistake could result in you having all your financials out of whack.

- ✓ Lastly, include some visuals. Show graphs and visual representations of your data to help the reader better understand it. You can also put supporting graphics in your appendix.

KEY Financial Projections

There are four basic kinds of financial statements that a business plan will usually include:

1. Balance sheet

2. Profit-Loss Analysis (Income Statement)

3 Cash-flow statement

4. Break-even Analysis

BALANCE SHEET

A balance sheet is a financial statement that shows the value of all assets, liabilities, and equity in a business. It shows the financial health of your business or project and is one of the main financial statements of a business plan, together with the profit and loss analysis and the cash flow statement. The balance sheet reflects your business' assets, liabilities, and equity.

How to Do the Balance Sheet

The basic equation for your balance sheet is that your **assets equal your liabilities plus your equity or your (or stockholders' equity.**

Assets = Liabilities + Equity.

A well-kept balance sheet is a key part of any successful project. It may seem tedious to make and update, or you may feel intimidated by the idea of it all, but the consequences of not having one or not maintaining one can be enough to break your business.

I will try to deconstruct what a balance sheet is and how to make and maintain your own.

Three essential components need to be listed on a small business balance sheet: assets, liabilities, and owner's equity. Assets refer to what your business owns and how much that's worth. Conversely, liabilities are what your business owes and how much that is worth. Finally, the owner's equity reflects the financial investments and any business partners.

This may seem simple enough, but it can be difficult to know exactly what to write down on a sheet and categorize it. Moving through the categories one by one, you'll learn exactly how to format your balance sheet.

ASSETS

Assets should always be listed first on your balance sheet.

Line 1 lists your business' cash account. Most businesses have cash on hand either to facilitate day-to-day transactions or they have cash on hand for emergency scenarios or situations where other forms of currency simply won't suffice.

Line 2 is for accounts receivable, money owed to you by customers and clients. This number will always be in-flux as you receive money from these individuals, or they accrue even higher debts with your business. The number reflected on your report is only expected to be accurate for the day it was created, and by no means do you need to keep it up-to-date daily.

Line 3 is for the inventory of your business. This line states the current value of the products you sell based on their market value and the quantity you possess.

The final line for assets is **Line 4**, reserved for fixed assets. Fixed assets are things your business owns and uses for operation, including land, buildings, vehicles, and equipment. The nature of fixed assets is that they are generally big-ticket items; you don't need to list every pencil and sheet of paper your company owns. Keep in mind that fixed assets generally depreciate over time. After all, you can't expect a company vehicle to hold the same value after several years of use.

All of your assets will be totaled on **Line 5**, representing the total value of everything your business owns.

LIABILITIES

This category is far less fun to tally up than the previous one, but it's still key!

Line 6 is accounts payable, the polar opposite of accounts receivable. This line represents short-term debts you have with any suppliers or manufacturers you work with. Much like accounts payable, these fluctuate frequently are only expected to be accurate as you publish your balance sheet.

Line 7 shows the total amount of loans you've taken out. Unlike accounts payable, these are long-term debts, often from a bank that last for more than a year. Many businesses use loans to stay afloat or to accommodate expansion.

EQUITY

Equity is listed in the same category as liabilities as it is money invested into the business.

Line 8 shows how much money has been invested by the owner and any other investors with a stake in the company.

Line 9 totals both liabilities and equity. The combined number should match Line 5, your total assets. If the numbers are not balanced, your balance sheet is not correct. A company cannot own more than it owes. Take another look through your files and see if you've missed something.

Here's an example balance sheet to help you visualize what yours should look like:

Assets	Value
1. Cash	$25,000
2. Accts Rec	$300,000
3. Inventory	$175,000
4. Fixed Assets	$500,000
5. Total Assets	*$1,000,000*
Liabilities and Equity	**Value**
6. Accts Payable	$ 120,000
7. LT Bank Loans	$280,000
8. Owner's Capital	$600,000
9. Total Liability + Equity	$1,000,000

INCOME STATEMENT

Income statements are a key part of effective recordkeeping for a business. They show whether your company has been profitable or not over a set timeframe. You can set the timeframe of your income statement to be whatever you please, but the most common timeframes are a month, a financial quarter, or an entire year.

"Profit and loss statement" is another term for this type of record, which should give you a better idea of exactly what it is. We'll break the process down line by line to know exactly how to format your income statement properly.

Line 1 is for your gross revenue. This means the total amount of money you've made in sales, including sales made on credit that has not been collected yet. If you sold 50,000 units of a product at $50 a unit, then your line 1 would read $2,500,000.

Line 2 is the cost of goods sold. This refers to all costs directly incurred by your product. Expenses of this nature include the cost of manufacturing, raw materials, and labor related to the product. This line is usually the highest cost for any business.

If the 50,000 units you sold in line 1 were bought during that same timeframe for $25 a unit, then that cost would be reflected in this line with a total of $1,250,000.

Line 3 is for your gross profit. Gross profit is simple to calculate. All you have to do is subtract line 2 (cost of goods sold) from line 1 (gross revenue). In our example this would be $1,250,000 ($2,500,000 - $1,250,000).

Line 4 represents your office expenses. This category focuses on selling, general, and administration fees (S, G & A) and any expenses not directly related to the sale of your product. S, G & A factors in wages, commission, rent, legal fees, accounting fees, and the like.

Utility costs such as electricity, heating, etc., can be included in this line or listed on a separate line as "utilities."

For our example, we'll list our expenses at $250,000

Line 5 is where your company's depreciation expense is listed. This line expresses the depreciating value of equipment and buildings owned by your company. This expense is primarily listed for tax purposes. Our example statement lists the total as $100,000.

Line 6 is for your operating profit. Operating profit is easily determined by subtracting lines 4 and 5 (office expenses and depreciation) from line 3 (gross profit). This number is more commonly known as the earnings before interest and taxes (EBIT). In our example, this line would read $900,000.

Line 7 is for interest expenses. This tracks interest that has accrued on debts held by your firm. Calculating interest is a simple matter of multiplying the interest rate of your debt by the principal amount of that debt. In our example, the interest is shown to be $50,000.

Line 8 is for earnings before taxes, and it is deduced by subtracting line 7 (interest expenses) from line 6 (EBIT).

Line 9 is the cumulative amount you pay in taxes. This covers federal, state, local, and payroll taxes. We're listing the total cost of taxes as $35,000.

Line 10 is where you list the earnings available to common shareholders. This is calculated by subtracting line 9 (tax expenses) from line 8 (earnings before taxes).

Line 11 is specifically for companies that hold investors and/or companies wherein the owner derives a salary from the profits. This line denotes the draw/dividend for these individuals

Line 12 represents your net income, which can be reinvested into the company. This number is found by adding all your expenses and then subtracting them from line 3 or more easily by subtracting line 11 (draw/dividend) from line 10 (earnings available to shareholders).

This is a basic example of an income statement. Your income statement may be more complex and have more lines depending on what expenses you run.

Remember that your income statement is only as accurate as the data used to compile it, so be sure to be rigorous in recordkeeping. Below is the example statement to help you visualize your own.

1. Gross Revenue	$2,500,000
2. Cost of Goods Sold	$1,250,000
3. Gross Profit	$1,250,000
4. Selling & Administrative Expense	$250,000
5. Depreciation	$100,000
6. Operating Profit (EBIT)	$900,000
7. Interest	$50,000
8. Earnings Before Taxes (EBT)	$850,000
9. Taxes	$30,000
10. Earnings Available to Common Shareholders	$820,000
11. Dividends/Owner Draw	$25,000
12. Net Income	$795,000

Cash-flow statement

Just like the income statement, the cash flow statement reflects your business' financial performance over a specific time. However, the income statement includes non-cash items like equipment depreciation or other assets. It may not be as practical as the cash flow statement if you're a solopreneur who isn't looking for outside investment, but if you are seeking investment, then it's essential. It is also useful for your accountant to do this anyway, as It can affect how much tax you have to pay at the end of the financial year.

Cash flow statements are integral to maintaining accurate finances. They're arguably more accurate than a profit and loss forecast, and they are especially helpful in determining whether or not your business can survive.

Essentially, a cash flow statement lists all of your incoming profits and outgoing expenses on a month-to-month basis.

This means everything from loan payments to personal investments into the business to standard cash and credit transactions. You'll be recording expenses in the month they occur rather than spreading them throughout the year. After all, if certain fees come due in September, then you'll need to know that you have the cash to pay them in September.

The advantage of this particular form of recordkeeping is that you'll know what months cost the most for your business to operate in and what months promise the greatest profits. You can adjust your costs accordingly, and if you find yourself coming up short in a month, you have time to take out a loan or seek alternative means of keeping things running.

Setting up a cash flow statement can be broken down into four simple steps.

1. Opening Balance

Your starting balance is exactly what it sounds like. The capital you have at the start of the month. This will likely be how much money you have in your business account in your first month of operations.

2. Projected Income

It's impossible to know exactly how much income you're going to make in any given month. That said, accurate projections can be made based on historical sales data and market research.

When calculating income, be sure to account for sales made on credit, which might not necessarily go through in the same month the sale was made. With that in mind, you must also account for sales made on credit in the previous month that will come through in the current month. Keeping cash and credit sales on separate lines in your cash flow statement can help you to get a clearer picture of where your sales stand.

3. Projected Expenses

This is essentially the reverse of step two. Instead of looking at the money going in, you'll be looking at the money going out. This includes all regular payments your business makes to stay running, including things like the cost of inventory, rent for any properties or equipment, loan payments, taxes, and any other costs you may incur in any given month. These costs should be much easier to account for than your profits as they should be relatively stable from month to month.

4. Total Income and Expenses

Subtracting your total monthly expenses from your total monthly income will tell you if you're profitable or not for that month. The figure you end up with is also the number you'll use as your beginning balance for the next month's cash flow statement.

If you find your total value at the end of the month is in the negatives, then you're going to have to re-evaluate your finances. Knowing what factors bring and take away money from your business and when they do so is the key to figuring out how to fix or improve your business. Be sure to consider non-obvious factors, such as how much inventory you carry and equipment you may be leasing.

Simply put, to get your cash flow back in the positive, you have to either increase the amount of money coming in or decrease the amount of money going out of your business. Ideally, you'll be able to manage both. Increased revenue can come from simply increasing sales. Consider a sale or promotional deal, but remember you'll have to sell more products if you lower your prices. Reduced expenses can come from finding different suppliers or reducing the labor you use. Additionally, a general reduction in the inventory and equipment you use can bring costs down a great deal.

Below is an example of what a cash flow statement might look like.

Cash Flow Analysis							
	January	February	March	April	May	June	July
Beginning Balance	5,000	3,340	3,080	2,220	1,960	1,700	-740
Cash Income							
Sales Paid	7,500	7,500	7,500	7,500	7,500	6,000	6,000
Collections of Credit Sales	2,000	2,000	2,000	2,000	2,000	1,600	1,600
Loans & transfers	0	0	0	0	0	0	0
Total Cash In	9,500	9,500	9,500	9,500	9,500	7,600	7,600
Cash Expenses							
Inventory	4,500	4,500	4,500	4,500	4,500	4,500	4,500
Rent	1,000	1,000	1,000	1,000	1,000	1,000	1,000
Wages	4,000	4,000	4,000	4,000	4,000	4,000	4,000
Utilities	100	100	100	100	100	100	100
Phone	30	30	30	30	30	30	30
Insurance	1,200	0	0	0	0	0	0
Ads	200	0	0	0	0	280	0
Accounting	130	130	130	130	130	130	130
Miscellaneous	0	0	600	0	0	0	0
Loan payments	0	0	0	0	0	0	0
Taxes							
Total Expenses	11,160	9,760	10,360	9,760	9,760	10,040	9,760
Cash at End of Month	3,340	3,080	2,220	1,960	1,700	-740	-2,900

Accounting & Finance Vocabulary Explained

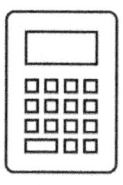

The terminology in the accounting and finance industries can be daunting for those unfamiliar with it. With so many terms and abbreviations flying around, how do you know what's essential?

ACCOUNTING PERIOD

The *accounting period* is the time during which you carry out accounting activities. It's usually measured in months, quarters, or years. The accounting period is particularly useful for investors since shareholders and prospective investors can evaluate a business's financial health by looking at accounts that are always connected to a specific time frame.

- An *accounting period* is a financial year or a calendar year usually, but it can also be a specific week, month, or quarter, in some cases, etc.
- The objective of an *accounting period* is to report and analyze. However, one isolated accounting period is often not enough, as it can be misleading. The accrual method of accounting provides consistent reporting so that people can get a more accurate idea of a business's financial health by seeing its performance over time.

- The *matching principle* aims to add transparency to accounting periods. It states that costs should be reported in the accounting period when they were incurred and that the revenue generated from those costs should be reported in the same accounting period.

Annual Report

A company's annual report for the stockholders includes financial statements that show how well operations have gone. It also reports any changes in ownership and important events affecting them, such as merger talks or an IPO announcement—anything relevant enough to include could be highlighted here! An IPO announcement is when a company announces that they intend to offer shares for sale on the stock market. It stands for Initial Public Offering.

Fiscal Year

A fiscal year is twelve months (consecutive) chosen by an entity as its accounting period. This may or may not be a calendar year, depending on the company's choice.

Accounts Payable

Accounts Payable are all the expenses that have been incurred by a business but that have still not been paid. These accounts show up on your Balance Sheet as an unpaid liability-a debt owed from the company to creditors for goods or services received in exchange for money changing hands. In other words, outstanding debt that is due.

Accounts Receivable (AR)

A company's uncollected revenue from prior customer purchases. This can be recorded on either the Balance Sheet or Statement of Cash Flows, depending on how it will eventually transform into cash for that entity in question.

Administration

Management of a company's finances from A-Z. This includes everything from how much money to spend on advertising to what fees will be taken with each purchase.

Acquisition

A company takes over from another by acquiring a controlling interest in it.

Asset

Assets are a company's most valuable resource. They represent the fruits of past transactions and events and anything legally claimed by the business, such as money or property rights in another person's name (like intellectual properties). An asset is something with economic value to its owner; it has future benefits too!

Audit

Professional scrutiny of a company's financial statement by an accountant or group to determine that it has been presented fairly. The purpose is for investors, creditors, and other parties involved in the transaction process to have confidence when using this information about what happened financially during their period with the said firm. It also serves to verify if anything may be off.

Balance Sheet (BS)

A balance sheet is a financial statement that shows the value of all assets, liabilities, and Equity.

Break-Even Point

The break-even point is where total revenues are equal to total costs. It's an essential concept because it can help you figure out whether or not your business will be profitable, at least in the short term.

Cash Flow

Cash flow is the money that enters and leaves a business. The Net Cash Flow for a period can be found by taking the Initial Cash Balance and subtracting the Closing Balance.

CREDITOR

The creditor is someone who loans money or other assets to another party. The borrower must agree in writing and pay back the debt, usually with interest at fixed intervals over periods set up by the agreement.

DEBTOR

The debtor is someone who owes money or other assets to creditors.

DEPRECIATION (DEP)

Depreciation is the term that accounts for a loss of value in an asset over time.

INCOME STATEMENT

The Income Statement, known as a Profit and Loss statement, is the second of two joint financial statements. It helps us understand how much money was made or lost by a business during their fiscal period - usually from January 1st through December 31st each year (or any other date if specified).

INTERIM PROFIT STATEMENT

An interim statement is a financial report for less than one year. Interim statements do not need to be audited and can help companies convey their performance before regular full-year reporting cycles without worrying about consistency, accuracy, or completeness with annual statements; this makes them an excellent tool for quick updates on important issues that may arise between now and then such as changes in inventory levels due to new product releases, etc.

Invoice Factoring

Invoice factoring is a great way to increase cash flow. You can sell all or some outstanding invoices at a reduced rate. The advantages are that you get instant access to cash, and you no longer have to chase up the invoices. The downside is that you pay a fee for this.

Negative Equity

Negative Equity occurs when property value falls below what is owed on it. Equity can be calculated by simply taking the current market price and subtracting that from how much you owe.

Operating Expenditure (Operating Costs) (OPEX)

Operational expenditure is a cost incurred by a firm due to its routine operations. OPEX is a common abbreviation; it includes equipment, inventory, marketing, and step costs.

Operating Profit/Loss

Operating Profit is the key to understanding a company's true profitability. A net income derived from operations eliminates several extraneous factors that can obscure its actual performance. Hence, operating profit or loss accurately represents their financial success, customer satisfaction, and employee retention rates.

Present Value

Present value, or PV for short, is the current worth of a future sum based on an assumed rate of return.

Return on Investment

The measure of profit a business makes through its basic operations. ROI is generally an indicator of management effectiveness. Calculated by dividing Net Income over Total Assets.

Rate of Return

Knowing the Rate of Return is essential when investing. The higher, the better! The ROR or Rate of Return of an investment is the net value of discounted cash flows once you've subtracted inflation.

FREE BUSINESS PLAN TEMPLATE

Access your **FULL FREE Business Plan Template** here:

https://www.idmbusinessenglish.com/free-business-plan-template

Get FREE Access to Training + Other Resources here:

www.idmbusinessenglish.com

INVESTMENT TERMS EXPLAINED

(DIGITAL COMPANION BOOK)

Sign up to the FREE VIP List today to grab your FREE downloadable Digital Book ☺

I hope you have found this book useful. Thank you for reading.

https://www.idmbusinessenglish.com/free-ebook-investment-terms-explained

CHAPTER 4. GRAPH VOCABULARY

When you describe a graph for a client, manager, or another stakeholder, you will need to use language to communicate changes, comparisons, and contrasts.

In this chapter, we'll focus on expanding your range of vocabulary and grammar structures for describing changes that can take place in a graph.

EXERCISE

Connect the vocabulary of change with the parts of the graph. More than one option is possible in some cases.

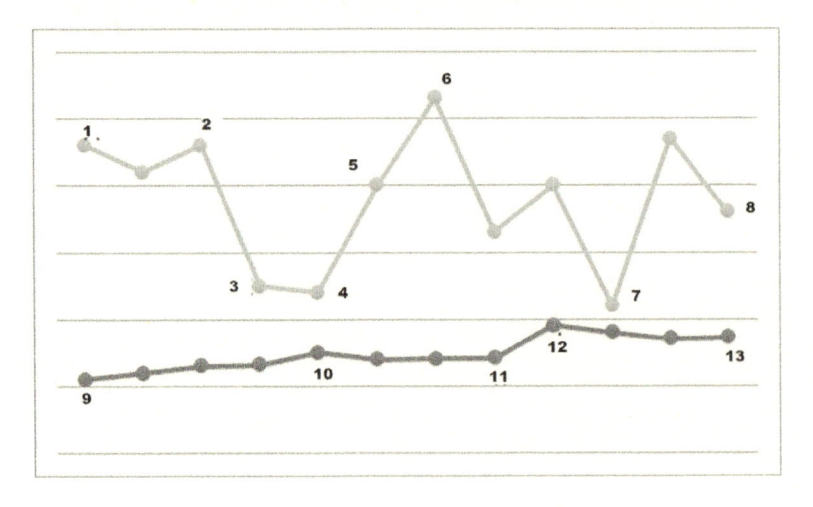

Rose steadily or increased steadily	Rose dramatically or increased dramatically	Rose gradually or increased gradually
Plummeted to or Plunged to ...	Hit a peak of, or Peaked at, or reached a high of ...	Fluctuated, varied, or oscillated
Dropped/ Shrank/Fell drastically/ sharply dramatically	Remained flat/unchanged/stable / constant at	Dropped and then leveled off/evened out at
Hit a low of .../ bottomed out at	Dropped and then quickly recovered	Dipped / Declined slightly before quickly

		recovering
Rocketed / Soared	Fell slowly/ gradually / steadily	Was erratic/ inconsistent

1-2 ....

2-3 ....

2-4 ....

4-6 ....

6 ....

6-8 ....

7 ....

9-10 ....

10-11 ……………..

12-13 ……………..

Definitions for some difficult words

Word	Explanation
Dipped	Fell slightly but recovered quickly
Bottomed out / Hit a low of	The lowest point on the graph
Plummeted to.../ Plunged to	Suffered a quick, drastic, or shocking decrease. Fell extremely quickly. A very quick and large drop or reduction
Fluctuated/ was erratic	Increases and decreases randomly, irregularly, or unpredictably
Rose/increased dramatically/ Soared/ Rocketed	Increased very quickly and drastically
Peaked at / reached a	The highest point on the graph

high of	
Remained constant/unchanged/ stable at ..../ Levelled off/evened out at ...	a part of the graph where there is no change

ANSWERS

1-2 Fell and then quickly recovered / Dipped/ fell slightly

2-3 Fell/dropped/shrank drastically/ dramatically / sharply/ Plummeted to/Plunged to

2-4 Dropped and then leveled off/evened out at

4-6 Rose/increased dramatically/Soared/ Rocketed

6 Hit a peak / Peaked at/reached a high of

6-8 Fluctuated/ was erratic

7 Hit a low of ...

9-10 Rose/increased steadily/ Rose/increased gradually

10-11 Remained flat/constant/unchanged/stable at

12-13 Fell gradually / steadily

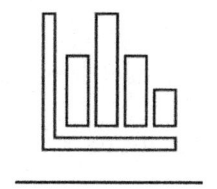

CHAPTER 5. BAR CHART

VOCABULARY

Bar Chart Language

When you talk or write about bar charts, you need to present the connections between the different parts of the chart or graph. You can do this by contrasting and comparing the information presented where necessary.

In most cases, you will not be using the language of change to describe bar charts. Instead, you will be comparing and contrasting the information.

	Example	Comparative	Superlative
1 Syllable	High/Low/ Cold/Wet	Higher/Lower/Colder/Wetter	The highest/lowest/ coldest/wettest
3 or more syllables	Effective/ Popular	More Effective/ Popular	The most effective/ popular
Ending in -y	Healthy/Early	Healthier/Earlier	The healthiest/ earliest
Irregular adjectives	Bad/ Little (for quantity)	Worse/ Less	The worst/ least

Remember:

1. Comparatives are made with *more* or *-er*, but NEVER both.

*The weather is getting **warmer**. (NOT ... more warmer.)*

*The game is getting **more popular**. (NOT ... more popularer.)*

2. Use superlatives to compare people and things with the groups or categories they belong to.

Mary is the tallest of the five girls. (NOT Mary is the taller of the five girls.)

James is the oldest person in the class.

Transitions

1. The UK imports close to 40 million tons of chocolate per year, <u>but</u> it produces only (a mere) 2% of the chocolate sold in Europe.

2. Spain produces large amounts of olive oil. <u>In comparison</u>, Italy produces very little.

3. China consumes more than a quarter of the world's meat. <u>On the other hand</u>, Germany consumes just 1.2% each year.

Subordinating Conjunctions

whether/ as much as/ once/ whereas/ that/ which/ whichever/ after/ as soon as/ as long as/ before/ by the time/ whom/ now that/ since/ till/ until/ when/ whenever/ while/ than/ though/ although /who/ whoever/ rather than/ whatever/ even though

1. China consumes more than a quarter of the world's meat, <u>while/whereas</u> Germany consumes just 1.2% each year.

2. <u>While</u> Germany consumes nearly 80 million tons of rice per year, it produces none.

3. *Though Italy produced over 6 million tons of olives, Spain produced almost double during the same period.*

Here are some structures for discussing similarities:

India consumes almost 100 million tons of rice per year; Likewise/ Similarly, China consumes 118.8 million.

Austria produced the same amount of butter as Switzerland in 2019.

Like Thailand, Malaysia produces 30,000 bottles.

Both the UK and Spain produce medium levels of carbon emissions.

CHAPTER 6. PIE CHART

VOCABULARY

You have to demonstrate a variety of language to keep your audience engaged. When describing pie charts, a variety of fractions and percentages are good. You should also use phrases to show when a number is not exact. Language like 'roughly,' 'just under,' or 'just over' are great in this type of description.

Here are some language examples to increase your flexibility when describing pie charts:

Percentages & Fractions

5% /   one in twenty

10% /   one in ten

15% /   under one fifth (to express that this figure is small)

15% /   almost one fifth (to express that this figure is large)

20% /   one fifth

25% /   one quarter

30% / under one third (to express that this figure is small)

30% / nearly one third (to express that this figure is large)

35% / over one third

40% / two-fifths

45% / over two fifths

50% / half

55% / over half

60% / three-fifths

65% / two-thirds

70% / seven in ten

75% / three-quarters

80% / four-fifths

EXERCISE ONE

Choose a qualifier from the list below and use it with a fraction to express the percentage on the left. The first one has been done for you as an example. You won't need to use all the options.

just over/just under/ almost / approximately/ ~~nearly~~/ over

Percentage = Qualifier + Fraction

74% = *nearly three-quarters*

48% =

15.5% =

63% =

69% =

ANSWERS

Percentage = Qualifier + Fraction

48% = just under half/ almost half

15.5% = approximately one fifth

15.5% = approximately one fifth

63% = over three-fifths / almost two thirds

69% = almost seven in ten

EXERCISE TWO

Pie Charts which Compare Past and Future

Use the lists of words 1-4 below to write your own sentences to describe a pie chart. Add the relevant data in brackets and change the verb tenses accordingly.

Diesel cars/account for (32%)/ traffic volume/ in 2019/ but/ in 2030/ forecast/represent (1%).

Estimate/success/rate/2021/(16%)/in contrast/to (29%)/2020.

in/ 2019/ smartphones/ make up/ bulk/ devices/ (82%) used/ but/ 2031/ this forecast/ drop to (30%)

....

....

....

....

Answers

1. Diesel cars accounted for 32% of traffic volume in 2019, but in 2030 they are forecast to represent 1%.

2. It is estimated that return on investment will fall to 16% in 2021 in contrast to 29% in 2020.

3. In 2019, smartphones made up the bulk of devices used (82%), but by 2031, this is forecast to drop to 30%.

CHAPTER 7. BUSINESS DATA

PRESENTED IN TABLES

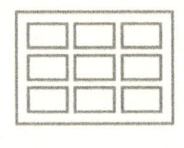

3 Important Points

1. You don't need to learn any new language to describe a table in a business setting successfully.
2. You need to look for data you can group when you start, as you would do in any other description.
3. Always start with the most relevant information (often the biggest things) and leave the least interesting data until the end of the description.

EXERCISE ONE

Re-write sentences a-i using the language in the box below. You can make any necessary changes.

There are four extra expressions you won't need to use.

- The bulk of
- the lowest percentages
- was noticeably higher
- a smaller proportion of
- was significantly higher
- had the lowest percentages
- had slightly higher figures
- a third of the number of
- 40% of
- Over 75%
- Three times the number of
- the largest proportion of
- One in four

A. The first training day was attended by three times as many people as the second.

B. More than four out of ten people chose to use trains.

C. The largest proportion of purchases came from Germany as opposed to Spain.

D. A quarter of customers ordered print rather than digital products.

E. The website lost just under three-quarters of its visitors compared to last year.

F. Consumers in all countries spent more on toys than any other product category.

G. Consumers spent the least on leisure/education in all countries.

H. Consumers in Turkey and Ireland spent much more on food, drinks, and tobacco than consumers in other countries.

I. Spending on clothing and footwear was a lot higher in Portugal, at 10%, than in other countries.

A. ....
   ....
B. ....
   ....
C. ....
   ....
D. ....
   ....
E. ....
   ....
F. ....
   ....
G. ....
   ....
H. ....
   ....
I. ....
   ....

SUGGESTED ANSWERS:

A. The first training day was attended by **three times the number of** people of the second training day.

B. More than **40% of** people chose to use trains.

C. **The bulk of** purchases came from Germany as opposed to Spain.

D. **One in four** customers ordered print rather than digital products.

E. The social media website lost just **under 75%** of its visitors compared to last year.

F. **The largest proportion** of spending in all countries was on toys.

G. The leisure/education category has **the lowest percentages** in the table.

H. Consumer spending on food, drinks, and tobacco **was noticeably higher** in Turkey and Ireland than in other countries.

I. Spending on clothing and footwear **was significantly higher** in Portugal, at 10%, than in other countries.

CHAPTER 8. PRODUCTION PROCESSES

Describing Sequences

The following linking words and phrases in the box **can** describe a sequence.

before / prior to	At first / firstly/ initially
following that/ after that / next / then/ when	as soon as/ once / immediately after/ in turn
before	after
where	At the same time- simultaneously
finally	

Exercise One

Highlight or underline the linking words in A-G and decide which is the first step in the sequence. Once you have done this, decide what is described and put the sentences in order.

A. If it's being refurbished, the faulty components of the device are repaired in the factory

B. and the tablet is then returned to the shop as a refurbished product.

C. Once the device breaks, it is either discarded or refurbished.

D. They are then assembled at a different factory

E. First, the computer processors for the tablets are manufactured in an outsourced factory.

F. Then they are sent to the central warehouse for distribution around the country

G. Simultaneously, the exterior and the memory chip are produced.

Exercise Two

Match 1 to 6 below with a sentence or phrase A-F to complete sequence descriptions. Please note that each full sentence belongs to a different process description.

1. As soon as the bricks have been formed
2. After fermentation,
3. Once the oranges are ripe, they are collected,
4. The water then flows into the penstock, which is a narrow chamber,
5. When the plant reaches a certain width, the leaves are picked.
6. In the early stages of milk production, cows graze in the field and are subsequently (then afterward) taken to a milking machine twice a day.

A. the chocolate is placed into molds and left to cool down.

B. The raw product is then heated to a high temperature to kill bacteria and make it safe for human consumption. Following this, it is put into refrigeration storage.

C. and they are then spread (laid) out on a large (industrial-sized) tray to enable them to dry under the sun.

D. they are left to dry.

E. they are then dried, sorted, blended, and packaged, ready for distribution to retailers.

F. and increases the pressure until the turbine turns.

Answers

Exercise 1

Linking words: if, and, then, once, then, first, simultaneously.

The lifecycle of a tablet computer is being described.

E, G, D, F, C, A, B

Exercise 2

1d, 2a, 3c, 4f, 5e, 6b

Some Essential Vocabulary for Processes

Noun	Verb
Storage	Store
Pasteurization	Pasteurize
Harvest – harvesting	Harvest
Delivery	Deliver
Assembly	Assemble
Packing -Packaging	Pack - Package

EXERCISE THREE

Read the process described on the next page and fill in the blanks with the missing word or phrase.

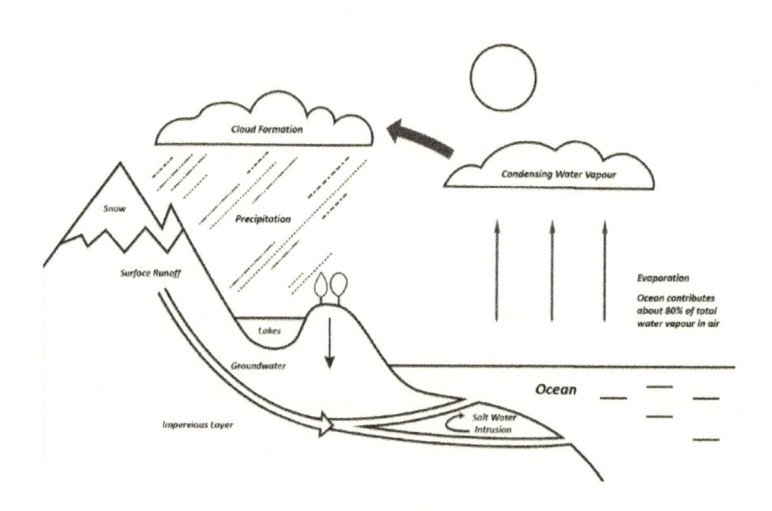

Diagram adapted from Nasa

https://gpm.nasa.gov/education/water-cycle

The diagram .... the water cycle. Firstly, water .... from the sea and floats into the atmosphere, ... **(two words)** accumulates in clouds and cools and condenses into

170

rain or snow. The next stage shows the water's journey after falling to the ground, ... ends with .... **(three words)**

In the first stage of the ...., water, approximately 80% of which comes from Oceans, ... into the air as a result of the heat of the sun. After ...., the water vapor condenses to form clouds. An .... 80% of the water vapor comes from Oceans.

In the next ...., as clouds accumulate condensation, they produce precipitation in the form of rain and snow. A large part of the water from the precipitation falls into lakes or is .... by the ground.

The groundwater then .... back to the ocean without reaching the impervious layer through surface runoff.

................., Ocean water seeps through to the freshwater aquifers during the process is saltwater intrusion.

ANSWERS

The diagram **illustrates** the water cycle. Firstly, water **evaporates** from the sea and floats into the atmosphere, **where it** accumulates in clouds and cools and condenses into rain or snow. The next stage shows the water's journey after falling to the ground, **which** ends with **saltwater intrusion**.

In the first stage of the **process**, water, approximately 80% of which comes from Oceans, **evaporates** into the air as a result of the heat of the sun. After **this**, the water vapor condenses to form clouds. An **estimated** 80% of the water vapor comes from Oceans.

In the next **stage**, as clouds accumulate condensation, they produce precipitation in the form of rain and snow. A large part of the water from the precipitation falls into lakes or is **absorbed** by the ground.

The groundwater then **flows** back to the ocean without reaching the impervious layer through surface runoff.

Finally, Ocean water seeps through to the freshwater aquifers during saltwater intrusion.

CHAPTER 9. MAPS, TERRAINS & LAND DEMOGRAPHICS

Verbs to describe changes in maps

EXERCISE ONE

Match each beginning of a sentence 1-7 with an ending A-G. More than one option may be possible.

Notice the verb phrases underlined in A-G (we will look at these later).

1. The center of the village
2. Several old houses
3. A new hospital
4. The old factories
5. Some old mills
6. Some of the trees around the old park
7. The fire station
8. <u>replaced</u> the old run-down sports center *
9. <u>were knocked down</u> <u>to make way for</u> a new park.
10. <u>were pulled down</u>, with a new hotel <u>taking their place</u>

11. <u>were demolished</u> <u>to create</u> more space which <u>was turned into</u> a campsite

12. <u>were chopped down</u> in order <u>to increase the size of</u> the path.

13. <u>was converted into</u> a gym and the car park <u>torn down</u>.

14. <u>was totally transformed</u> over the fifteen-year period.

*run-down is an adjective that means decaying, dirty old, and not taken care of.

Useful change phrases for map descriptions:

Replaced	took the place of
were knocked down to make way for	when a building or wall is deliberately destroyed to create space for something else
were pulled down	building or wall destroyed because it was very old or

	dangerous
were demolished to create	when a building or wall is deliberately destroyed to create space for something else
was turned into	were transformed or changed into something else
were chopped down	the action of cutting trees until they fall
to increase the size of	generic term for: *to make bigger or wider*
to reduce the size of	generic term for: *to make smaller or narrower*
taking their place	occupying the place where the other thing used to be
was converted into	was transformed or changed into

| was torn down | was knocked down |

EXERCISE TWO

Underline the most appropriate verb in bold in sentences 1-8 and put it into the right form to suit the sentence.

1. The abandoned car park near the woodlands **develop/become** into a museum.
2. The area around the city center **turn into/become** less accessible with the construction of the new theatre.
3. As the city **extend/expand**, more bus stations were built.
4. A bus station **construct/ become** after the old warehouses were knocked down.

5. The downtown area of the city completely **change/demolish** with the introduction of the new shopping center.
6. A number of important developments **take place/convert**, which totally **alter/expand** the character of the premises.
7. The area **turn into/become** more family-friendly with the **introduce/ knock down** of new parks and open spaces.
8. The road was **extend/expand** to the town center, and a new bus service was introduced to carry passengers to and from the airport.

....

....

....

....

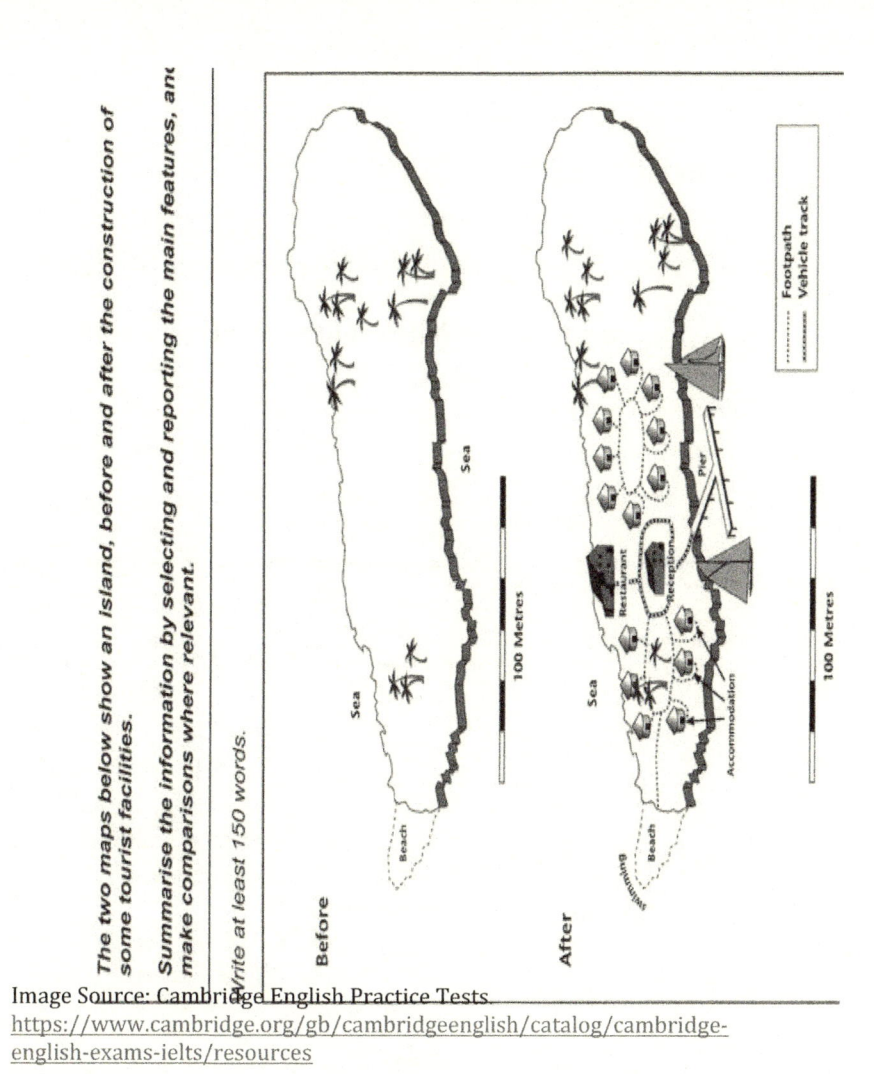

The two maps below show an island, before and after the construction of some tourist facilities.

Summarise the information by selecting and reporting the main features, and make comparisons where relevant.

Write at least 150 words.

Image Source: Cambridge English Practice Tests.
https://www.cambridge.org/gb/cambridgeenglish/catalog/cambridge-english-exams-ielts/resources

EXERCISE THREE

Look at the following map. Read the sample answer on the next page and fill in the blanks with the missing word or phrase.

> The two maps below show an island, before and after the construction of some tourist facilities.
>
> Summarise the information by selecting and reporting the main features, and make comparisons where relevant.

Write at least 150 words.

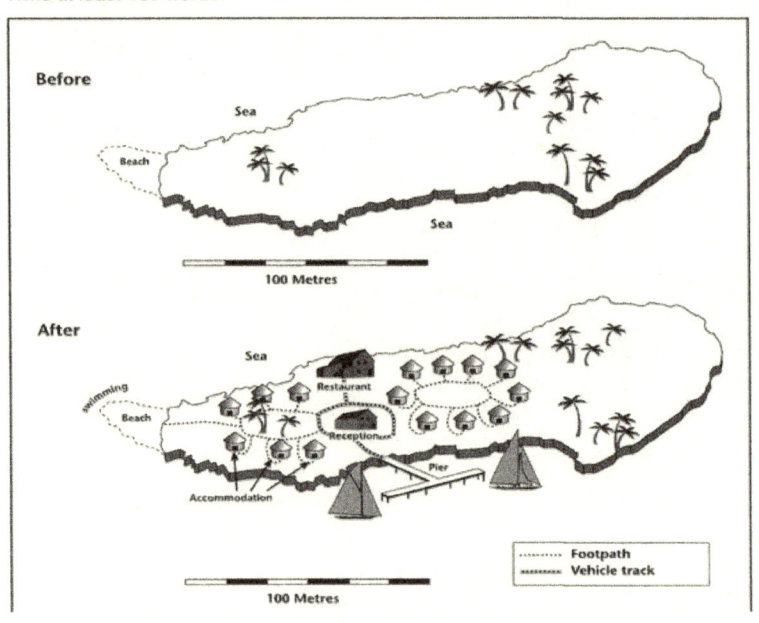

Before — Sea, Beach, Sea, 100 Metres

After — swimming, Sea, Beach, Restaurant, Reception, Accommodation, Pier, Footpath, Vehicle track, 100 Metres

Image Source: Cambridge English Practice Tests.
https://www.cambridge.org/gb/cambridgeenglish/catalog/cambridge-english-exams-ielts/resources

Sample Description

The two maps illustrate the changes which have .... **(two words)** on a small island, prior to and after its development for tourism.

The introduction of tourism on the island has .... **(two words)** the landscape, with several new developments that can be seen in the second diagram. The most important changes are that the island now has ample accommodation for tourists, and there is a peer to enable visitors to access the island.

One of the most striking changes is the accommodation huts which are connected by footpaths and which have been .... around the reception and restaurant area. A total of 6 huts have been constructed in the west of the island, and another nine have been built around the center of the island.

A pier has also been developed on the south coast of the island to make the island .... to tourists, and there is a short road linking it with the reception and restaurant. The trees scattered around the island have been left untouched, and a swimming area has been .... just off the beach.

Answers

Exercise 1

G

B/C/D

A

B/C/D

B/C/D

E

A/F

Exercise 2

developed/was developed

became

expanded

was constructed

was completely changed / completely changed

took place, altered

became, introduction

was extended

Exercise 3

The two maps illustrate the changes which have taken place on a small island, prior to and after its development for tourism.

The introduction of tourism on the island has significantly changed the landscape, with several new developments that can be seen in the second diagram. The most important changes are that the island now has ample accommodation for tourists, and there is a peer to enable visitors to access the island.

One of the most striking changes is the accommodation huts which are connected by footpaths and which have been built around the reception and restaurant area. A total of 6 huts have been constructed in the west of the island, and another nine have been built around the center of the island.

A pier has also been developed on the south coast of the island to make the island accessible to tourists, and there is a short road linking it with the reception and restaurant. The trees scattered around the island have been left untouched, and a swimming area has been designated just off the beach.

CHAPTER 10. MEETINGS & PUBLIC SPEAKING

Connecting words and set phrases

Putting your reasons in order	Firstly/Secondly. Thirdly/Finally
Expressing an opinion	I hold the view that ... In my view... It is probably true to say that.... There can be no doubt that ...
Mentioning what other people think	It has been suggested that.... There are those who believe that... There are those who argue that... Opponents/ supporters of (e.g., hunting) ... argue that....

	Most people hold firmly to the belief that… It is often claimed that…
Common opinions in society	It is widely believed/thought that Few people would contest that…. Nobody would dispute the fact that …. It is generally agreed that…
Referring to evidence and facts	Research suggests that… All the evidence suggests that … Recent evidence indicates that …..

Changing direction	However/Nevertheless
Giving examples	For example for instance such as
Concluding	In conclusion / Overall,

EXERCISE ONE

Read the beginning of the presentation. Fill the gaps with an appropriate word or phrase from the box (You don't need to use all of them):

To conclude	I hold the view that	however.	Firstly, research suggests that
may	which can lead to	For instance,	when people
they are more likely to	Secondly, few people would contest that	Therefore	it is likely that
Finally,	such as	However, there are those who	nobody would contest the

192

			argue that	fact that
In addition, it is often claimed that	Nobody would dispute the fact that		there can be no doubt that	Hence,

1. .... many government initiatives create inefficiencies .... gaps in the market.

2. .... we should be investing more in trying to exploit these gaps in the market, ... many people disagree with this opinion. In the next 30 to 40 minutes, we will examine the issues, and I will try to convince you that we are currently missing out on some of the biggest opportunities available in the

sector. *(Note: to **miss out on** means when you don't take advantage of an opportunity)

3. ....,(a) ....(b) over 70% of government initiatives create new inefficiencies, and that the companies in the sectors which could solve these new problems take an average of 12 months to react.

4. .... last year's biggest projects all came from problems caused by government initiatives; we lost three contracts that we could have won if we had approached the clients sooner. If we can provide agencies with early, reliable information and solutions .... react positively and award us the contracts.

ANSWERS

1. **Nobody would dispute the fact that** many government initiatives create inefficiencies **that can lead to** gaps in the market.

2. **I hold the view that (a)** we should be investing more in trying to exploit these gaps in the market, **however (b)** many people disagree with this opinion. In the next 30 to 40 minutes, we will examine the issues, and I will try to convince you that we are currently missing out on some of the biggest opportunities available in the sector. *(Note: to **miss out on** means when you don't take advantage of an opportunity)

3. **Firstly, research suggests that** over 70% of government initiatives create new inefficiencies and that the companies in the sectors which could solve these new problems take an average of 12 months to react.

4. **For instance**, last year's biggest projects all came from problems caused by government initiatives; we lost three contracts that we could have won if we had approached the clients sooner. If we can provide agencies with early, reliable information and solutions, **they are more likely to** react positively and award us the contracts.

REFERRING TO PREVIOUS INFORMATION

Here is an example of how we can use this structure in a presentation, email, or report.

The words in the box below are useful examples of words like 'argument,' which you can use with the word 'this' (or 'these' in plural) to specify more information.

analysis	approach	concept	context
data	definition	environment	evidence
factor	issue	problem	function
measure	method	period	policy
principle	procedure	process	theory
response	sector	structure	interpretation

Here is an example of how we can use this structure in an essay.

There is no doubt that corruption is the most important point to focus on here because it originates from positions of power. Corruption can take many shapes and forms, such as political, which involves crimes in a country's legal system and within the police, and economic, for example, by misusing tax money. All the evidence suggests that countries with corrupt governments cannot develop as quickly as countries with less corruption.

These factors [...].

OR

This negative environment [...].

The first sentence of a paragraph is vital, as it shows how it connects with the overall structure and can signal what will happen next.

Pro Tip:

When you practice writing, always check that your text is logical by underlining the most important sentences in each paragraph. You should understand the whole text only by reading those sentences. If you can't, you need to make changes.

CHAPTER 11. WRITTEN BUSINESS COMMUNICATIONS

LETTER OF REFERENCE

In this type of formal letter, you're asked to provide a reference for a colleague or friend to a prospective employer or educational institution.

You may find it helpful to note down useful expressions which you can include,

Some Useful Language for this type of letter or email

I have known X for ....

I am confident that ....

I have no hesitation in recommending him ....

X is sociable, reliable, self-confident, outgoing

X possesses a thorough grounding in ...

stand him in good stead

as is shown by the fact that ...

EXERCISE ONE

Look at the gaps in the sample answer below:

Where could you use these linking words and discourse markers to complete the text? You will not need to sue all of them.

Firstly, in addition, for instance, moreover, furthermore or by way of example.

Sample Answer (Letter of Reference):

To whom it may concern,

Mary and I worked together at J&J Retail for ten years.

It is my pleasure to recommend her for the position of Shop Assistant.

1......................., Mary is a self-confident and outgoing person who finds it easy to relate to people from all kinds of backgrounds.

During her time at J&J Retail, Mary proved to be friendly, communicative, hard-working, and excellent at managing her time. 2...................., Mary is the kind of person who works well with others, as she displays great sensitivity and sympathy. She was always willing to contribute and help her colleagues. 3................... at J&J Retail, she was popular and fully committed to the organization's objectives.

4.................... at J&J Retail, Mary demonstrated excellent English language skills dealing with English-speaking customers daily. She passed her English exams around six months ago and has a keen interest in fashion, which I am sure will stand her in good stead when she is helping customers in English.

I recommend Mary without reservation — she would be an excellent asset to your company.

Please do not hesitate to contact me if you have any questions.

Sincerely,

Now you can check your answers by reading "Sample Answer (Letter of Reference)" on the next page...

SAMPLE ANSWER (LETTER OF REFERENCE):

To whom it may concern,

Mary and I worked together at J&J Retail for ten years.

It is my pleasure to recommend her for the position of Shop Assistant.

Firstly, Mary is a self-confident and outgoing person who finds it easy to relate to people from all backgrounds.

During her time at J&J Retail, Mary proved to be friendly, communicative, hard-working, and excellent at managing her time. In addition, Mary is the kind of person who works well with others, as she displays great sensitivity and sympathy. She was always willing to contribute and help her colleagues. Moreover, (Furthermore) at J&J Retail, she was popular and fully committed to the organization's objectives.

By way of example, (For instance) at J&J Retail, Mary demonstrated excellent English language skills dealing with

English-speaking customers daily. She passed her English exams around six months ago and has a keen interest in fashion, which I am sure will stand her in good stead when she is helping customers in English.

I recommend Mary without reservation — she would be an excellent asset to your company.

Please do not hesitate to contact me if you have any questions.

Sincerely,

Your name and Surname

REFERENCE PRONOUNS

Reference pronouns like *this, that, they,* or *it* are commonly used to refer back to something or someone recently mentioned.

RELATIVE CLAUSES

Relative clauses can give added information to a statement, and they allow you to link ideas together in well-formed sentences.

SUBSTITUTION

Other forms of cohesive devices include things like substitution. This is where you use a synonym, for example, to refer backward or forward to a connecting point in the text.

E.g., Replacing a verb phrase:

The management team at J & J Retails were very happy with Mary, and so were the rest of the staff (and the rest of the staff were also very happy with her).

Using paragraphs and various cohesive devices effectively will help you score well in the "Coherence and Cohesion" and "Task achievement" parts of the assessment criteria. **Tip:** When you're reading, make a point of looking out for cohesive devices like the ones we've looked at in this section.

LETTER OF COMPLAINT:

I am writing to complain about...

I would like to express my dissatisfaction with ...

I am writing to express my concern about the....

I must complain in writing about...

I feel I must complain to you about...

I wish to complain in the strongest terms about...

I am writing to inform you of an apparent error in your records...

PARAPHRASING EXERCISE

Example:

0) Basic Problem: *"I want to complain about the bad service in the restaurant. "*

ii. Key Language: *I would like to express my dissatisfaction with ...*

iii, Key Word you must use: POOR (Bad is too informal so that we can use *poor* instead)

iv. Final Product: *"I would like to express my dissatisfaction with the poor standard of service in the restaurant. "*

Now try to complete the process using the following language:

1)

i. Basic problem: *"The cinema is far away from everything."*

ii. Key Phrase: *I wish to complain in the strongest terms about...*

iii, Key Word: ACCESSIBILITY

iv. Final Product:

....

....

2)

i. Basic problem: *"During my course, there were too many students in the class."*

ii. Key Phrase: *I am writing to express my concern about the....*

iii, Key Word: NUMBER

iv. Final Product:

....

....

Answers

1) I wish to complain in the strongest terms about the accessibility of the cinema.

2) I am writing to express my concern about the number of students in the class during my course

TOPIC-SPECIFIC PHRASES

• *Poor standard of service/slow service*

• *I am asking for/I would like to request a replacement*

• *No accommodation/Travel delays/Rather rude staff*

• *Badly scratched/dented wrapping/packaging*

• *To claim/demand for a refund*

• *I am returning ... to you for correction of the fault/for inspection/repair/servicing*

• *Defective/faulty goods/defective item/machine*

• *The... may need replacing*

• *To restore an item to full working order...*

• *I am enclosing the broken radio in this package; please send me a replacement.*

• *You said that ... I feel sure there must be some mistake as I am sure that...*

ENDING THE LETTER

• *I do not usually complain, but, as an old customer, I hope you will be interested in my comments.*

• *We look forward to dealing with this matter without delay.*

• *I feel that your company should consider an appropriate refund.*

• *I would be grateful if you would send me a complete refund as soon as possible*

•*We feel there must be some explanation for (this delay) and expect your prompt reply.*

• *Will you, please look into this matter and let us know the reason for ...*

- *Thank you for your assistance.*

- *I look forward to hearing from you at your earliest convenience.*

- *I am returning the damaged goods/items... and shall be glad if you will replace them.*

- *Please look into this matter at once and let me know the delay.*

- *Please check your records again.*

- *Thank you for your cooperation in correcting this detail...*

- *I wish to draw your attention to...*

- *I would suggest that...*

- *I suggest that immediate steps be taken.*

- *I wish to complain about...*

- *I look forward to a prompt reply and hope that you will take into consideration...*

- *I am dissatisfied with...*

Now, look at the example. Pay special attention to the language and structure used.

Sample Answer

Dear Sir/Madam,

I would like to express my dissatisfaction with the poor standard of service we received during our recent visit to Dino's Bar. Firstly, the staff members were generally quite rude and unhelpful, they seemed to lack basic food knowledge and did not seem interested in the job. For instance, none of them could offer any advice on choosing a dish.

A further cause for complaint was that the food was cold when it arrived at our table. I understand that it was a busy night, but we booked the table and the menus the day before, so they should have been ready.

Finally, not only did we receive substandard food and unfriendly, unhelpful service, but we were also charged full price for our meals after we complained. In my opinion, the prices seem to be very expensive for the quality of the food and the service provided.

I do not usually complain, but, as a loyal customer, I hope you will be interested in my comments. Perhaps it would be appropriate to offer some training courses to the staff at Dino's Bar to avoid this from happening again. I feel that customer service was a big issue, as was the food quality. If these two problems were fixed, then the price might not be such an issue in the future, as customers would be happy to pay a little more for a better experience. I hope you will take these points into consideration

I look forward to your reply.

Yours faithfully,

Name and Surname

FORMAL BUSINESS COMMUNICATION:

STRUCTURE RULES

Greeting

Name unknown: *Dear Sir/Madam,*

Name known: *Dear Mr.../ Dear Mrs... / Dear Ms..+ surname*

Reason for writing

I am writing to ... I am writing concerning...

I am writing on behalf of ...

Asking questions

I would be grateful if ... I wonder if you could ....

Could you ...?

Referring to someone else´s letter /points

As you stated in your letter, ...   Regarding .../ Concerning ...

With regard to ....

Finishing the letter

If you require any further information, please do not hesitate to contact me.

I look forward to hearing from you.

Signing

If Dear + name = Yours sincerely,

If Dear Sir/ Madam = Yours faithfully

Then, your first name + surname must be written clearly under your signature

FORMAL BUSINESS COMMUNICATION GENERAL CHECKLIST

When you have finished your message, check:

- ✓ It is formal communication.
- ✓ It includes all the information necessary
- ✓ You have asked all the questions you need to
- ✓ If it's written, check that the message is divided into paragraphs. If it's spoken, it should be divided into sections.
- ✓ You have checked carefully for mistakes

FORMAL BUSINESS COMMUNICATION: LANGUAGE EXERCISES

Letters can be anything from very formal to very informal. In this section of the chapter, we will focus on your use of language and, in particular, your ability to create a formal register.

At the end of this section, you will find a list of useful formal-informal equivalents. This list will save you a lot of time. For example, in a letter of complaint: *"I was rather disappointed"* is a formal way of saying *"I was furious"* or *"I was very angry."* See how many more formal and informal equivalent items you can learn next.

Exercise One

Transform each informal or semi-formal phrase into a formal phrase. You can make small changes to the content of the sentences if you think it's necessary, and you can use a dictionary.

Example: I thought I'd write = I am writing

a. state of the playground =

....

b. I have noticed loads of rubbish =

....

c. I reckon =

....

d. The teacher I'm talking about =

....

e. On top of this =

....

f. a load of problems =

....

g. You could =

....

h. stop = ...

i. What's more =

....

j. better = ...

k. To finish =

....

l. I´m looking forward to hearing from you =

....

Answers

a. state of the playground = condition of the playground

b. I have noticed loads of rubbish = There is a great deal of litter

c. I reckon = It is my opinion that...

d. The teacher I'm talking about = The teacher in question OR The teacher I am referring to

e. On top of this = Furthermore

f. a load of problems = a number of problems

g. You could = it may be possible for you

h. stop = prevent

i. What's more = In addition,

j. better = more suitable OR more adequate

k. To finish = In conclusion,

l. I'm looking forward to hearing from you = I look forward to your reply, OR I look forward to hearing from you

Exercise Two

Now here are some full sentences from formal letters. Complete the sentences using only one word.

a. I am writing in .... to your job advertisement in the ABC newspaper

b. I would like to .... for the position of Translator.

c. I am .... to go for an interview at any time convenient to you.

d. I would be .... if you could send me further information regarding the position.

e. Please find my CV ....

f. I would like to express my .... with the poor standard of service we received during our recent visit to your cinema.

g. For ...., none of them could offer any advice to me on choosing a dish.

h. Finally, not only .... we receive substandard food and unfriendly, unhelpful service, but we were also charged full price for our meals after we complained.

ANSWERS

a. I am writing in reply/response to your job advertisement in the ABC newspaper

b. I would like to apply for the position of Translator.

c. <u>I am available/ able to go</u> for an interview at any time convenient to you.

d. I would be grateful if you could send me further information regarding the position.

e. Please find my CV attached (email)/ enclosed (letter).

f. I would like to express my dissatisfaction with the poor standard of service we received during our recent visit to your cinema.

g. For instance, none of them could offer any advice to me on choosing a dish.

h. Finally, not only did we receive substandard food and unfriendly, unhelpful service, but we were also charged full price for our meals after we complained.

USE THE PASSIVE (SOMETIMES)

The next example is where the passive has been used instead of an active form. This is a common feature of formal writing but should not be overused.

This sentence is an example of how we might structure a sentence formally.

Informal: *"The waiter did offer us another dish, but when it arrived, it was cold again."*

Formal: *"Although we were offered an alternative dish when it was delivered to the table, it was cold again."*

Notice two clauses in the informal version are joined by **but** whereas in the formal version, the two clauses have been reversed and **but** is replaced with **although,** which starts the sentence. This is a more formal way of saying the same thing.

Within the formal sentence, *"Although we were offered an alternative dish, when it was delivered to the table it was cold again,"* there are further examples of vocabulary that is more formal than the equivalent in the informal version. For example, an *alternative dish* is a more formal way of saying *another dish*.

As we saw above, phrasal verbs are most typical of informal letters —although some have no more formal equivalents and are common in all types of letters (*look forward to,* for example). However, most phrasal verbs do have formal equivalents, and these would be preferred in most formal letters, whereas the formal equivalents would be very rarely used in an informal letter.

6 Quick Rules of Formal VS Informal:

1. We tend to understate our feelings and say *I was rather disappointed* or *somewhat surprised* instead of saying how we really felt.

2. For the same reason, we do not use exclamation marks.

3. We often use the passive to emphasize the action when the person is of less importance

4. We avoid contractions in formal letters.

5. We use formal equivalence of idiomatic language and phrasal verbs

6. Particular sentence structures can be used to create a formal tone. Inversion is one example of this "Although we were offered an alternative dish when it was delivered to the table, it was cold again."

EXERCISE

Rewrite the following sentences using formal equivalents for the phrasal verbs. Use a dictionary if necessary. You might need to make other changes to the structures.

1) I'm so chuffed that you've been talked into coming to the meeting.

……………………………………………………………………

……………………………………………………………………

2) The football club's facilities have been done up, so this should make our performances better.

……………………………………………………………………

……………………………………………………………………

3) As our town is quite cut off, perhaps we could arrange for you to be put up in a hotel in the city for a few days.

....

....

4) We will make up for the inconvenience of having to wait for so long.

....

....

Answers

1) I am very happy that you have been convinced to attend the meeting.

2) The football club's facilities have been refurbished, which should improve our performance.

3) As our town is relatively isolated, we could arrange hotel accommodation in the city for a few days.

4) We will compensate you for the inconvenience of having to wait for so long.

LINKING WORDS

LINKING MARKERS

	Openers	**Conjunctions**	
	Co-ordinating		**Subordinating**
ADDITION	In addition [to NP], ...	...and ...	, who...
	Moreover, ...	not only ...,	, which...
	Also, ...	but also ...	, where...
	Apart from [NP], ...		, when...
	Furthermore, ...		
CONTRAST	However, ...	... but ...	although...
	Nevertheless, ...	...(and) yet...	whereas...
	On the other hand, ...		while...
	In contrast, ...		in spite of the fact tha
	In spite of [NP], ...		despite the fact that...
	Despite [NP], ...		
CAUSE/	So...	...(and) so...	so...
EFFECT	As a result...	...(and) hence...	so that...
	Consequently...		because...
	Therefore...		due to the fact that...
	Thus...		
	Hence...		
	For this reason...		
	Because of [NP],...		
POSITIVE	In that case,...	...and...	if...
CONDITION	If so,...	...and (then)...	as/so long as...

Note: [NP] = Noun Phrase, which may include a noun or a verbal noun (-ing form):

e.g., Instead of <u>complaints</u>, it would be better to offer advice

Instead of <u>complaining,</u>

EXERCISE

Rewrite the information below in 3 or 4 sentences. You must decide how the ideas are logically related and then use a marker or conjunction (coordinating or subordinating) to match your meaning.

Learning French is not easy. Many people would argue that learning Spanish is harder.

French and English share a lot of similarities in their vocabulary. French and Spanish both have different articles for masculine and feminine nouns. You have to change the endings of adjectives to match the nouns. This is hard for speakers of English. English does not use adjective endings.

Most people believe that speaking English helps you to start learning French and Spanish. When you have passed the basic stages, English is less helpful. At an advanced level of Spanish and French, knowing English is arguably not very helpful.

Answers

Learning French is not easy, but many people would argue that learning Spanish is harder because French and English share a lot of similarities in their vocabulary. Nevertheless, French and Spanish both have different articles for masculine and feminine nouns. Therefore, you have to change the endings of adjectives to match the nouns, which is hard for speakers of English since English does not use adjective endings. Most people believe that speaking English helps you to start learning French and Spanish, but when you have passed the basic stages, English is less helpful and at an advanced level of Spanish and French, knowing English is arguably not very helpful.

INFORMAL BUSINESS EMAILS & LETTERS

An informal email should contain very friendly, very simple, straightforward language.

LET'S START WITH AN EXAMPLE TASK.

A colleague from a different office is visiting your region for a couple of weeks during his holidays and has written to you to ask for several recommendations.

Write an email to your colleague

In your email, you should:

• offer to help find accommodation

• give advice about things to do

• provide information about what clothes to bring...

In this type of task, you should begin your letter as follows:

Dear ... your colleague's first name.

A few things to keep in mind.

• You should have at least 150 words. Aim for about 180 (a little bit more but don't go too long- If you're over 240 words, you've written much more than you need to.)

• Address the points have your opening and closing, and that's it!

• Address the points have your opening and closing, and that's it!

Let's start with the general idea of what you're trying to do, what you're trying to accomplish.

The tone:

'The tone" of the letter or email means how your letter sounds or the overall feeling it gives the reader. It should be very relaxed, very informal.

For example: if you're writing to your friend or close colleague, write it as though you were speaking; very casual.

You can start with:

Dear- Hello- Hi and then the person's first name, never their surname.

You shouldn't use *Mr., Mrs., Dr...*

Do not put first and last names because you do not address people by their first and last name in informal situations.

Use contractions:

Now contractions are suitable. So in terms of how you're going to use *I've, it's, doesn't, etc...* In a formal email, you say *do not,* whereas, in an informal email, you say *don't.*

Slang and idioms

Not only are slang and idioms okay now, but they're recommended because they create a feeling of closeness and friendliness in the right situation. However, remember it must be natural, so don't be too heavy on the slang or the idioms. One or two idioms here and there are great, but if you overuse them, it becomes unnatural.

Note that you can use idioms in your formal emails as well but very carefully, very selectively, and it has to be very appropriate, so it's generally not recommended.

Stay organized and focused:

You still have to remember what you're doing and make it very clear in the email. Are you thanking the person, are you answering a question, are you asking for something, are you offering advice? Make this clear right away in the introduction. Make sure the body follows.

Language

Again, you don't want to use formal language in an informal email; you don't want to use too many formal or complex words because that's not how we usually communicate.

In social situations, we're usually very casual and relaxed.

For example:

I just wanted to say thanks for helping me out last week.

In a formal email, you would write

I'm writing to express my appreciation and gratitude for your assistance with last week's matter...

Notice the different feel of the two sentences. One is very casual; one is very formal.

Another example:

Should you require any further information, please do not hesitate to contact me - formal.

<u>Versus</u>

Let me know if you need anything else - super casual.

CHAPTER 12. ESL BUSINESS ENGLISH

If you are not a native English speaker, this section will be helpful. We will be looking at some common phrasal verbs that people use in business and some commonly confused words in business writing.

Important Phrasal Verbs for Business Communication in All Settings

What is a phrasal verb?

Phrasal verbs are two or more words that perform the same function as another verb. A phrasal verb is a phrase made up of the main verb and an adverb, a preposition, or both. They are idiomatic ways of expressing an action. Think of it like a sandwich:

[Main Verb] + adverb/preposition/adverb and preposition = phrasal verb

Phrasal verbs are unique to English and other Germanic languages and can cause issues for English learners. They can be transitive (they take a direct object), intransitive (they do not take a direct object), separable (they can be separated), and inseparable (they cannot be separated). Later on, we will cover the differences between these, complete with descriptions and exercises.

Although the meanings differ, phrasal verbs are conjugated just like main verbs. For example, to break down conjugates like to break:

The car breaks down.

The car broke down.

Here are some common phrasal verbs to get you started:

Phrasal Verb   bring up

Example *He brought up the fact that I was too short to go on the rollercoaster.*

Meaning: to mention a topic

Phrasal Verb   call off

Example *She called off the wedding.*

Meaning: to cancel

Phrasal Verb   carry on

Example *The bag was heavy, and my feet hurt, but I carried on with the walk.*

Meaning: to continue

Phrasal Verb   deal with

For example, *I can't deal with stress.*

Meaning: to handle

Phrasal Verb   end up

Example *They ended up in Sheffield.*

Meaning: to reach a state or place

Phrasal Verb   fall through

Example *Our plans to meet for coffee fell through.*

Meaning: to not happen

Phrasal Verb   get on with (something)

Example *She was busy, so I got on with the end-of-year accounts.*

Meaning: to continue to do

Phrasal Verb   hand in

An example *I handed in my thesis.*

Meaning: to submit

Phrasal Verb   join in

Example *She joined in the conversation at the party.*

Meaning: to participate

Phrasal Verb   keep up with

Example *My boss talks too fast, and I can't keep up.*

Meaning: to stay at the same pace or level.

Phrasal Verb   let down

Example *She was supposed to collect me at 6:00, but she didn't. She really let me down.*

Meaning: to disappoint

Phrasal Verb   look forward to

Example *Are you looking forward to your holiday?*

Meaning: to be excited about something, to anticipate something good.

Phrasal Verb   mix up

For example, *I can't tell the twins apart; I always mix up their names.*

Meaning: to mistake one thing for another

Phrasal Verb   pass away

For example, My grandfather *passed away last night.*

Meaning: to die

Phrasal Verb   put off

The example *I kept putting it off, even though I knew I had to do it*

Meaning: to postpone

Phrasal Verb   rule out

Example *We know it wasn't John who ate Sarah's pasta so that we can rule him out*

Meaning: to eliminate

Phrasal Verb   stick up for (someone)

For Example, *Catherine was constantly getting bullied, so Alex stuck up for her.*

Meaning: to defend

Phrasal Verb   think over

For example, *Janine told Roger that she would have to think over his proposal.*

Meaning: to consider

Phrasal Verb   work out

Example

1. *It's important for your fitness that you work out three times a week.*

2. *The Math problem was complex, but I eventually worked it out.*

Meaning:

1. to do physical exercise

2. to solve a problem

EXERCISE ONE

Try to match the phrasal verbs below with their synonyms:

Phrasal Verb   *Example*

a. throw away   *John threw away his apple core.*

b. look into   *Sarah looked into the murder case.*

c. get away with   *The robber got away with the crime.*

d. use up   *Use up the washing-up liquid before you buy another bottle!*

e. run out of   *My phone ran out of battery.*

Meanings:

1. use completely

2. exhaust supply

3. investigate

4. discard

5. escape blame

Check your answers at the end of this chapter.

When can I use Phrasal Verbs?

Phrasal verbs are used in non-formal and semi-formal situations. You will hear them used in speech daily, in business articles, in emails between work colleagues, memos, meetings, presentations, seminars, and conferences. They are extremely common, but there are certain situations where you should avoid using them:

- Very formal letters or emails.

- Academic papers

EXERCISE TWO

In the following email, underline all the phrasal verbs that you can find and write their meanings below. You may need to use a dictionary.

Hi Jack,

I'm sorry that I was late to work today. My car broke down yesterday, so I took the bus instead. However, the bus was held up in traffic! It seems that everyone was going to work at the same time!

Don't worry about the project; I'll be able to catch up with the rest of my colleagues. I'll drop by the office on the weekend and see if there is anything extra that I can do.

I hope you've got over your cold; I hear it's been going around the office recently.

Best wishes,

Gary

(1)   /

(2)   /

(3)   /

(4)   /

(5)   /

(6)   /

ANSWERS

Exercise 1:

a) 4

b) 3

c) 5

d) 1

e) 2

Exercise 2:

(1) break down / to stop working

(2) hold up / to delay (to be held up to be delayed)

(3) catch up / to do tasks

(4) drop by / visit briefly

(5)   get over / to recover from an illness

(6)   go round / to affect a lot of people

Commonly Confused Words in Business Writing

Affect – influence (verb)

Effect – a change (noun)

Poor time management can affect your work performance.

Poor time management can have a significant effect on your work performance.

Whether – this is used to show an alternative in an indirect question

Weather – the condition of the atmosphere in an area

I'm not sure whether the project should go ahead.

I'm sure that the meeting is going to go smoothly tomorrow.

Uninterested – when someone is bored by something or doesn't have any motivation to pay attention to it.

Disinterested - neutral

She is obviously uninterested in this job; she makes minimal effort to learn anything new.

I think journalists should be impartial representatives of public opinion.

Loose – not fixed or contained.

Lose – to experience defeat or to misplace something

These trousers are too loose; I need a size smaller.

We cannot lose that client. We have to fix the problem quickly!

Cite - to quote a source of information

Sight – the ability to see. Also, "a sight" is something that can be seen.

Site – a place

It's important to cite a variety of sources in your marketing reports.

He lost his sight in one eye in his old age.

This would be an excellent site for the new factory.

Allowed – permitted

Aloud – to speak in a voice loud enough for others to hear

We are not allowed to leave the house during the quarantine.

He was visibly nervous as he read the words aloud.

Comprise - consist of or be composed of.

Compose - to constitute

The new office comprises ten meeting rooms and two bathrooms.

The new office is composed of ten meeting rooms and two bathrooms.

Accept - agree to receive or do something

Except - preposition meaning 'not including.'

I would like you to accept the job.

All her colleagues attended the meeting except Kelly.

Elicit – to bring out or provoke a reaction.

Illicit – illegal or frowned upon

The presenter elicited answers from the audience before explaining the solution.

The director was suspended pending an investigation into his alleged participation in illicit activities.

Imply - To express something without saying it directly

Infer – to come to a conclusion based on the evidence available

He was implying that she could not handle the job.

From what she said, we were able to infer that she had the situation under control.

Incredible – impressive, astonishing

Incredulous – unsure, or not believing something

The size of the new project is incredible.

He was incredulous when he first heard about the size of the new project.

Historic -a standout event in history.

Historical – related to history.

Columbus set sail with his team of Spanish explorers in his historic voyage, searching for China and India.

I donated some historical reference books to the local library last week.

Assert - to affirm.

Ensure - to make sure

Assure - to try to reduce someone's fear or worry by saying something positive

She asserted that there was financial espionage going on.

We wanted to ensure that the project would be finished before the deadline.

She assured us that the project would be completed on time.

Complement – to add to or complete something

Compliment – to give praise

The sauce complements the meat perfectly.

The financial director complimented John on his handling of the crisis.

BUSINESS ENGLISH ESL VOCABULARY:

CONVERSATIONS (SPEAKING PHRASES)

Likes/dislikes	Opinion
I'm into…	As far as I'm concerned,
I'm a keen/avid (surfer)	As I see it,
I'm keen on/fond of	From my point of view,
I like nothing more than to start a new project	In my opinion,
	I'd say that…
I'm itching to try/go…. (I really want to)	
Comparing/contrasting	**Describing something**
Both adverts show…	The first thing that strikes me about this project is…
They look as though they are….	
Whereas/while in this picture…	The thing that really jumps out is…
In contrast	
On the other hand	In this project, it looks as if/though they are…
	They could/might/they

	may be… They could/might/may have just… I'm pretty sure that they're feeling… I'd guess that they are…
Agreeing We see eye to eye. Yeah, I'd go along with that. Absolutely! You took the words right out of my mouth. I couldn't agree more. You have a point there. I'm with you 100% on this one.	**Disagreeing** We don't see eye to eye. I take your point, but… I tend to disagree with you there. That's not always the case I beg to differ Isn't it more a case of…
Starting to make a conclusion or decision Let's get down to the nitty-gritty. The bottom line is we have to choose one…	**Asking for opinion** What's your take on….? Where do you stand on….? In my opinion…., would you go along with that?

It's a tough one; I'm torn between ... and .... Shall we go with ....?	What are your thoughts on this?
Personalizing Speaking from personal experience,... For me personally,... This is a topic that is particularly close to my heart... It's funny. I was just thinking about this the other day. My gut/initial reaction is... If I were to choose one of these options, I'd go with... because...	**Impressive structures** Another point I'd like to add about ... is... It's also worth bearing in mind that... Coming back to what (James) was saying about .... I'd also like to point out that... I think it's important not to forget that... The vast majority of people tend to think that... At the end of the day... When all's said and done...
Tips	**Asking for repetition**

Eye-contact Active listening Open body language Speak up Don't dominate too much	I beg your pardon. I didn't catch that. Sorry, would you mind repeating that, please? Could you repeat the question, please?

CHAPTER 13. LEARN 2,500 NEW BUSINESS WORDS IN 6 MONTHS.

Do you spend a lot of time and effort learning vocabulary but still find difficulty using it when required? Have you spent a lot of time memorizing vocabulary words but forget them when you need them the most? Don't worry if you answered a big resounding "YES" to any of these questions because you are not alone. Several valuable tools, methods, and exercises will have you not only remembering but using your extended vocabulary with minimal effort. Let's get started!

Method 1: Mnemonic Devices

What are mnemonic devices? Well, they include a variety of techniques and methods that help remember or recall information.

Method 2: FANBOYS

For example, many students often need to recall the conjunctions used in English grammar. Remembering FANBOYS is an excellent tool to recall these words (For, And, Nor, But, Or, Yet, So). The best part of this is using your creativity to make it exciting and different. You could create a song out of the words, similar to what many children do when they learn the names of countries and capitals. Finding some words that rhyme together would give your song some rhythm, so get creative and don't be afraid to try something a bit silly. Silly is good because it helps the brain remember.

METHOD 3: THE TONGUE TWISTER METHOD

Tongue twisters are a fun way of practicing sounds, and this repetition of sounds creates another type of rhythm: *Silly Sally sat by the seashore collecting seashells.* This is a tongue twister for children, but the principle remains the same.

This can be done with words that begin with the same sound or have similar sounds within or at the end of a word. It can create an exciting beat or jingle, which helps you remember easily and quickly.

METHOD 3: TEACH THE MIRROR METHOD

One of the best and easiest ways to remember anything is to teach someone else. If you can't teach someone else, teach yourself in the mirror!

Share your knowledge. To teach vocabulary to someone else, you need to have a good grasp of the word and the many contexts in which it is used. If you refer to a dictionary, you may find multiple definitions related to the word itself. Before teaching, it's crucial to study and thoroughly understand the word first. Look for sentences that contain that word, so you can understand how it can be used. Practice making your own sentences as well. Encourage the "student" to ask questions for understanding and clarity.

METHOD 4: HACK YOUR ROUTINE

Now it's essential to use what you have learned. As the saying goes: "If you don't use it, you lose it." The first step here is to look for ways to use the new words.

Method 5: Notecards or post-it notes

Notecards or post-it notes are as helpful as they are handy. You can stick post-its anywhere as a reminder. Just write the name, short definition, or even a sentence as an example. Here's what your notecard could look like:

Impart: to make known

Synonyms: tell, disclose

Sentence: Teachers impart knowledge to their students.

Method 6: Use Suffixes

Suffixes are word endings that may change a word's meaning. They can be used to change a word so that it maintains the rules of grammar. Consider the following sentences

It is a tradition in Chinese culture to eat using chopsticks.

The older generation is more traditional than today's youth.

A priest traditionally conducts the wedding ceremony.

Learning suffixes and how they change words is a valuable tool. With the suffix -ally, as in "traditionally," it is understood that we are using an adverb describing an action. The –tion in "tradition" makes it a noun, so it's often placed at the beginning of a sentence. Understanding the placement of words will help you make sure sentences are grammatically correct.

METHOD 7: READ, READ, AND READ!

Today's fast-paced lifestyle makes it challenging, if not impossible, to make time to read. However, it's essential. Read things you enjoy or find useful, don't force it. If you like music, read about music; if you like business, read business!

METHOD 8: THE 30-MINUTE RULE

The 30-minute Rule states that thirty minutes of pleasurable reading every day will lead to excellent results in your level of English over time. 'Thirty-minute readers,' people who read for fun for at least 30 minutes per day, tend to have a vast vocabulary. Furthermore, several studies have suggested that the health benefits can be considerable: living longer, increasing IQ, and reducing stress, among other perks. Over time, reading regularly can also increase vocabulary and make it easier to utilize these words in practical and functional situations.

Look for friends or colleagues who enjoy reading. Interacting with bookworms or avid readers will often help you pick up vocabulary or new expressions. Don't hesitate to ask about anything unfamiliar.

METHOD 9: THE NEWSPAPER METHOD

Newspapers and news websites offer a wealth of information at your fingertips. Whether it's the paper version or the electronic version, it doesn't matter. Newspapers are a tool that will spark curiosity and encourage you to read more about a variety of topics.

METHOD 10: THE INTERACTION METHOD

Spend time interacting with expert professionals in various fields if you can.

That doesn't mean you need to spend time at colleges or universities. Expand your field of awareness and interest to connect to those outside your circle of friends and colleagues. You can join various chat forums or groups on social media.

Learn new vocabulary and subjects. You will see the difference.

METHOD 11: THE CHUNKING METHOD

NEVER write a single word followed by a definition in your notebook! Always add an example sentence and pay attention to the original sentence where you saw this word. English words can often change meanings depending on the prepositions they go with or the type of sentence they are in.

For example:

He was turned away at the door because he was wearing trainers.

Meaning: He was rejected

He turned away when I tried to speak to him because he was furious.

Meaning: He looked the other way or turned his head towards a different direction, so he didn´t have to look at me.

Pro-Tip

Make it fun!

Learning new English vocabulary words doesn't have to be a chore! Find ways to make it fun, enjoyable, and rewarding. Download a few gaming apps that focus on building or using vocabulary words. A common one is "Words with Friends," where you get to share and learn new words with your circle of friends. Try it! You will see the results.

FREE EBOOK: "COMMON INVESTMENT TERMS EXPLAINED"

Sign up to the FREE VIP List today to grab your FREE downloadable eBook ☺

I hope you have found this book useful. Thank you for reading.

https://www.idmbusinessenglish.com/free-ebook-investment-terms-explained

FREE BUSINESS PLAN TEMPLATE

Access your **FULL FREE Business Plan Template** here:

https://www.idmbusinessenglish.com/free-business-plan-template

Get FREE Access to Training + Other Resources here:

www.idmbusinessenglish.com/free-templates

THE END & SPECIAL THANK YOU

Thank you...

If you enjoyed this book or found it helpful, I'd be very grateful if you'd post a short review on Amazon. Your support does make a difference, and I read all the reviews personally, so I can get your feedback and make this book even better.

If you did not enjoy this book, OR, if you need any help finding the FREE templates, **please email us directly so that we can help!**

marc@idmbusinessenglish.com

Thanks for reading, and thanks again for your support!

Made in the USA
Las Vegas, NV
27 July 2023